A VERY BRITISH REVOLUTION

MARTIN
BELL

A VERY BRITISH
REVOLUTION

The Expenses Scandal and How to
Save Our Democracy

ICON BOOKS

This updated edition published in the UK in 2010 by
Icon Books Ltd, Omnibus Business Centre,
39–41 North Road, London N7 9DP
email: info@iconbooks.co.uk
www.iconbooks.co.uk

Previously published in the UK in 2009 by Icon Books

Sold in the UK, Europe, South Africa and Asia
by Faber & Faber Ltd, Bloomsbury House,
74–77 Great Russell Street, London WC1B 3DA
or their agents

Distributed in the UK, Europe, South Africa and Asia
by TBS Ltd, TBS Distribution Centre, Colchester Road,
Frating Green, Colchester CO7 7DW

This edition published in Australia in 2010
by Allen & Unwin Pty Ltd,
PO Box 8500, 83 Alexander Street,
Crows Nest, NSW 2065

ISBN 978-184831-128-2

Typesetting in Plantin by Marie Doherty

Printed and bound in the UK by
CPI Mackays, Chatham ME5 8TD

Contents

Martin Bell OBE is one of the best-known and most highly regarded names in British television journalism. As a BBC reporter he has covered foreign assignments in more than 80 countries and eleven wars including Vietnam, Nigeria, Angola, Nicaragua, The Gulf and Bosnia, where millions watched as he was nearly killed by shrapnel. In 1997 Martin became the first Independent MP to be elected to Parliament since 1950, and he has since campaigned tirelessly for trust and transparency in British politics.

His previous books are *In Harm's Way* (Penguin, 1995), *An Accidental MP* (Viking, 2000), *Through Gates of Fire* (Weidenfeld & Nicolson, 2003), and *The Truth That Sticks* (Icon, 2008).

Swindlers' List

I wish I had my own duck house,
Redacted and anonymous,
A shaded pool where ducks could float,
A pond, a river or a moat,
A place unto the manor born
Where moles would not uproot the lawn.
I was not born to privilege,
But loitered at the water's edge,
And played the Honourable Member
From January to December.
I wish to thank the voters' sense
For choosing me at their expense;
On their behalf I did my best,
Including things they never guessed.
Though my accomplishments were zero,
In fiddling I was next to Nero,
I was a self-philanthropist,
Master of the John Lewis List;
I had a profitable innings
And duly pocketed the winnings,
The subsidies, the perks, the pay,
The petty cash, the ACA.
The Tudor beams, the chandeliers,
The bills for swimming pool repairs,
The hanging plants, the trouser press,
Nothing exceeded like excess,
The whirlpool bath, the horse manure,
Whiter than white, purer than pure.
And so it was until, alas,
The MPs' scandals came to pass.
I was your Honourable Friend –
A pity that it had to end.
And then to avoid the sneers of Mr Paxman
I wrote a cheque and sent it to the taxman.

Introduction

We have been through a period of political revolution
the like of which we have not known in our lifetimes. It
has been very British and very peaceful, but nonetheless
profound. Its outcomes will permanently change the
nature of our politics and especially that of the House
of Commons. It has arisen from the publication of the
detailed expenses of Members of Parliament, which were
in most cases beyond reason and in some beyond belief.
They ranged from petty thieving to outright fraud. They
provoked what can perhaps be best described as a 21st-
century version of the Peasants' Revolt – an uprising of
the people against the political class and its practices and
patterns of corruption. Not all MPs were equally guilty.
Some were not guilty at all. But the corruption was
revealed to be widespread and pervasive. We have been
witnesses of something unique in its character and which
will, I believe, be positive in its consequences.

It was hard to know whether to laugh or cry: we did a
bit of both. 'Corruption,' said Peter Ustinov, 'is nature's
way of restoring faith in democracy.' Great reforms are
driven by great scandals. And this has been one hell of

a scandal. Not only have we lost faith in our politicians: they have even lost faith in themselves. So the perpetuation of the status quo is not an option for any of us. These events will be studied for years by those who will write the history of our insurrection. This book, which was written as it unfolded, is an attempted first draft of that history.

So rich is the seam of source material that when I told a friend about it, he asked: 'How many volumes?' Just one will do for the time being. Others may follow. The list of misdemeanours goes on and on. Not all the politicians caught up in the scandal have yet been driven from office. But it has changed the weather in Westminster, the style of political campaigning and the terms of trade between the parties. So it *is* a very British revolution. It has really started something.

Alan Duncan (Conservative, Rutland and Melton) was one of the MPs who found himself in the thick of it. Not only was he Shadow Leader of the House, and therefore responsible for his party's policy on MPs' expenses, but his own gardening costs were found to be on the high side, including £598 to overhaul a ride-on lawnmower. A protester had himself filmed digging a pound-shaped flower bed in Mr Duncan's lawn in Rutland and planting it with flowers. The video became an instant hit on YouTube. The MP wisely asked the police not to prosecute, and he said: 'The outpouring of fury we are witnessing is like a spring revolution.' But he also thought that at £64,000 a year MPs were underpaid and 'forced to live on rations'. The MP for Rutland and Melton was removed from the Shadow cabinet.

There are those who believe that the outpouring of fury will pass like a sudden storm, and that when it has passed they can carry on much as they used to. There are others who understand that it has changed our politics permanently. I am firmly in the second camp. We cannot return to where we were, which was the politics of the pig trough, because the people will not stand for it. The revolution will not be complete until all the rogues in the House are gone and public confidence in the MPs remaining is restored. The overhang of the scandal is so great that even new Members in a new Parliament will find themselves initially on probation. The restoration of public trust in public life will be work in progress, per-haps for many years. They will have to keep at it. And so shall we.

My only qualification for writing this account of the ongoing revolution is that I am a taxpayer and a true-believing democrat who was once an MP and a part of the Commons' system of self-regulation, the Committee on Standards and Privileges. I was there. I sat back and marvelled. I saw what worked and what didn't – espe-cially what didn't. For all its neo-Gothic grandeur, the House had something of the Wild West about it: too many villains, too few sheriffs, and laws that turned out not to apply to the regulars in the saloon bar. Even ten years ago, from the vantage point of Committee Room 13, the regular meeting place of the Select Committee on Standards and Privileges, I believed that the regulatory system, such as it was, would one day hit the buffers. I had no idea that the crash would be so sudden and spectacular. Some resigned and others were left clinging to the wreckage.

Sir Philip Mawer, Parliamentary Commissioner for Standards from 2002 to 2007, took a similar view. He told Sir Christopher Kelly's Committee on Standards in Public Life: 'The recent furore over MPs' allowances is a car crash which has long been waiting to happen. Not only has the reputation of many decent MPs but that of the "Mother of Parliaments" itself has been seriously damaged in the wreckage. ... The damage will take years to restore.'[1] He laid the blame on a collective failure of leadership in the House of Commons itself. MPs should have seen this coming, but fought shy of the reforms that were necessary to save their reputations.

This account of the scandal is therefore about more than moats and mole traps. It sets out to explain why and how the crash occurred. It looks ahead to the reforms that are necessary, in a House of Commons which will inevitably, because of its own shortcomings, have sacrificed some of its sovereignty and may yet need to sacrifice more. It analyses the half-measure of the Parliamentary Standards Bill. It draws on a variety of sources: my own experiences, conversations with some of my friends and co-conspirators in the House, contacts with politicians across the country, *Hansard*'s record of certain key debates, submissions to the Kelly Committee on Standards in Public Life, and the thousands of pages of the MPs' expenses themselves.

It also sets out an unexpected military dimension. A sharp increase in British casualties in Afghanistan coincided with the news of the widespread misconduct of the political class. It raised a question of integrity: in terms of the military deployments and resources allocated, how could we entrust the lives and futures of the men and women of the armed forces to MPs who had in so many cases proved to be untrustworthy in their personal affairs, had gone AWOL from their responsibilities and who had appeared to exercise their duty of care, in some cases, principally to their bank accounts? While the soldiers were losing lives and limbs, one of Labour's Defence Secretaries responsible for their welfare was walking away, over a four-year period, with £12,000 in petty cash. How can that make sense? Just work it out: or as the Americans put it, go figure.

I am obviously grateful to the *Daily Telegraph*, not only for its initiative in securing the documents that showed the extent of this misconduct, but for the thoroughness, even-handedness and sheer bloody-mindedness with which it presented them. Bloody-mindedness is a journalistic virtue. Day after day, the *Telegraph* and its Sunday sister paper just kept at it, and found gold in the silt that they sifted. They did us all some service. If we had relied on the 'redacted' records published by the MPs themselves, we would have had no idea of the extent of their misconduct.

My thanks also to Peter Cox of Redhammer, to Stevie Cook for her additional research, and to Peter Pugh, Simon Flynn, Andrew Furlow, Duncan Heath and

Najma Finlay of Icon Books. Thanks of a sort are also due to the MPs themselves, whose milking of the system was so extraordinary that the book took on a life of its own and almost wrote itself. It was a ten-week labour of love – and of doubt and dismay and incredulity. It was also a satirist's despair, since no parody could have matched the real-world story that unfolded.

From out of this shambles we have to find a way of rebuilding confidence and electing MPs who will deserve the trust of the people. There never was a golden age of parliamentary democracy; but some times have certainly been worse than others, and this is one of those times. What the House of Commons could be is one thing, and what is has become is quite another. It is not too large an ambition to hope for a Parliament to be proud of. So I shall place some signposts along the way. We are not, to be realistic, aiming for an unattainable state of grace, but at least for a politics of less disgrace than that in these past few years.

Chapter 1

Bath Plugs, Moats and Duck Islands

It began with an 88p bath plug.

The bath plug was bought by or on behalf of the Home Secretary Jacqui Smith, MP for Redditch since 1997. Along with the bath plug there were other items listed as necessary expenses, including a barbecue and a patio heater. They were all acquired for her constituency home, where she lived with her husband, who was her constituency assistant, and her two children. By any common sense definition it was her main home, since it was her family home and had been for many years; and it was where she was registered to vote. But one of the things we have learned about public life is that common sense flies out of the window when politics comes in through the door. She told the Commons authorities that her main home was her sister's house in south London, where she rented a room, and maybe a little more than a room, while working in Westminster. This allowed her to claim all the parliamentary allowances that were due, and some that were not (which she duly paid back), on her home in Redditch.

As it turned out, Jacqui Smith's residential arrangements, in which she switched her designated second home from one property to another, were by no means unique. Other MPs, and other cabinet ministers, did the same, sometimes two, three or even four times. This was because the second home, but not the main home, was subsidised by the taxpayer. The practice was known as 'flipping'. But it seemed remarkable, and even borderline, when the story came out in February 2009. We ordinary people – including even ex-MPs like myself – had no idea that this was going on. A complaint was made to the Parliamentary Commissioner for Standards, Mr John Lyon, that Jacqui Smith was in breach of the rules.

Mr Lyon was fifteen months into his post as Commissioner. Unlike his distinguished predecessor but one, Elizabeth Filkin, he was not a rocker of boats or maker of waves. But it will be remembered that Elizabeth Filkin was removed from the job in 2002, essentially for doing it too well. She made MPs uncomfortable by the thoroughness of her investigations; and only now do we know how much they had to be uncomfortable about, which was why they resisted. As Elizabeth Filkin observed, they had the opportunity to self-regulate and they subverted it very, very seriously. The SNP leader Alex Salmond, one of her small band of supporters in the Commons, called her departure a 'political assassination'. Mr Lyon was certainly aware of the precedent, although he never consulted her. He had a reputation in Whitehall as an official who went into his office, closed the door and stayed there. Besides, he was no more independent than any of the three Commissioners before him. They were servants of the House, and of its all-powerful Commission under the chairmanship of the Speaker. The House of Commons had always stood firm against outside regulation. The theory was that none was needed, since it was a gentlemen's club of 'Honourable Members' who could be trusted, at least by each other.

Mr Lyon initially ruled that he would not investigate the complaint against the MP for Redditch who, like so many others, appeared not to know where she lived. This seemed to me such an extraordinary decision that I wrote to him about it. I had no formal standing in the matter, since I was no longer an MP. But I was a taxpayer like millions of others and had once served on the Committee on Standards and Privileges, to which the Commissioner reports; so I knew how the system worked – or in this case didn't. I pointed out to him that previous Commissioners had experienced most difficulty with complaints against high-profile MPs, and hoped this wasn't happening again. I noted that the affair was damaging still further the reputation of the House of Commons, and was sure that he would not wish this to happen on his watch. I politely indicated that I thought he had made a mistake.

He wrote back to me immediately. He defended his decision to take no action, on the grounds that the complaint had been based only on a story in a newspaper,

The Mail on Sunday: 'After careful consideration, I concluded that the newspaper report did not provide me with sufficient evidence that Ms Smith had breached the rules. I came to my own independent conclusion, taking no account of Ms Smith's position in Government, and I hope without fear of the likely reaction from the press to this judgement.' But in the meantime he had received another complaint (from a neighbour of Jacqui Smith's in south London, about how often she actually stayed there) and had decided to investigate that.

Things then got worse for the Home Secretary. It emerged that she had made a claim of £10 for a cable TV service of two adult movies watched by her husband, Richard Timney. Mr Timney apologised and she paid back the money. It was a very public humiliation and clearly distressing for both of them and presumably for their family. There was a hidden dimension to the great public scandals of 2009, in which careers were ruined and reputations destroyed at the turn of a page: in every case they were accompanied by a great deal of private hurt. Innocent people, including children, were caught up in them. But it was the Member herself who had signed the mistaken expense claim. It was the personal pain that was caused by the episode, and the acres of adverse publicity devoted to it, that led Jacqui Smith to stand down as Home Secretary, though not as an MP. Inevitably she lost confidence in herself. She said later: 'I think I've had a harder time than some for less sin, because I was the first person for which there were questions about my expenses.'[2] She described herself as 'The poster girl for the expenses scandal'.[3] There has never been a time in our political life when so many MPs, one after the other, have had so much to regret in so short a space of time.

Throughout the spring and early summer the saga of swindles and scandals unspooled – leaving the voters bewildered, occasionally amused and finally extremely angry. The gravy train had left the tunnel and for the first time was out in the open for all of us to see. Many of the miscreants were long-serving MPs who had made a point in their election addresses of calling for thrift, economy and an end to waste in every corner of government. Now they were exposed as the biggest wastrels of all. They were switching homes to maximise the benefit. They were employing accountants to prepare their private tax returns at public expense. They were hiring their relatives and subsidising their families with taxpayers' money. They were furnishing their second homes, and even their first homes, with luxuries – an £8,000 television set here and a £600 array of hanging baskets there. They were especially keen on trouser presses. They were prodigious consumers of toilet paper. They were pocketing the petty cash. They were even charging for their grocery bills. One of them claimed for dog food and another, rather suitably, for pork pies. On their walls they were claiming for etchings and in their gardens for horse manure and mole traps. The extremists among them were using their allowances to develop an entire portfolio of properties. The spivs and speculators flourished. There was no limit to the feathers that lined their nests. The lists of their acquisitions went on and on. Democracy retreated and kleptocracy advanced.

It was both a national disgrace and a national joke; and it would have been even if the good times were still rolling. But they were not. It seemed that everyone except the political class was feeling the winds of the recession. Ordinary, blameless and decent people were losing their homes and their jobs. The point most frequently made against the Honourable Members was that in any other walk of life, like a private company or public corporation, they would have been handed their coats, escorted out of the door in short order and instructed not to return: the evidence of their wrong-doing might then have been passed to the police. Or if they were soldiers, risking their lives in distant lands on the politicians' orders, they could have faced a board of inquiry or court martial for a simple £10 discrepancy. The people were united in their outrage. From Luton to Totnes and from Scunthorpe to Bromsgrove, the universal complaint was: Why is there one law for them and another for us?

The most serious cases concerned actions which, outside the walls of the Palace of Westminster, would have been thought to fall within the categories of fraud, embezzlement and the misappropriation of public money. These involved MPs who had claimed reimbursement for mortgage payments long after the mortgages had actually been paid off, and others who had claimed for more than they actually owed. They said – they would, wouldn't they? – that the errors were inadvertent and made in good faith. They had just been too busy to notice. They were big-picture people. They were better with words than with numbers. Even the Chancellor and Shadow Chancellor, supposed to have expertise in these matters, came unstuck on the details of their claims. As for the Justice Secretary, 'Accountancy does not appear to be my strongest suit', wrote Jack Straw over a council tax error in his Blackburn constituency. This too was against all common sense. We all have to pay attention to the bottom line. When expenditure exceeds income we do not have the luxury of closing the gap at the tax-payers' expense. We cut our spending. Those of us who have been paying substantial sums to building societies for our mortgages for 30 years or more will not lightly forget the day when the payments cease. We have come through. A burden has been lifted from us.

Politicians live in a different world. When Peter Mandelson was under investigation by Elizabeth Filkin over his application for a mortgage on a house in London while not declaring, on the application form, that he had already taken out a loan on his home in Hartlepool, his answer was that *he did not know a mortgage was a loan.* And now he is the Wizard of Oz. And a peer of the realm. And other princely things.

I shall deal with the open-ended mortgages later. They caused quite a stir when they were first revealed. But to voters baffled by the intricacies of the MPs' rules, and especially the Alternative Costs Allowance for second homes, the eye-catching items that the MPs claimed for were the little things that people could more easily relate to in their own lives: bath plugs, light bulbs, toilet seats and mole traps among others. (The mole traps were John Gummer's.) Then came the rather bigger things, like whirlpool baths (Celia Barlow MP) and mock Tudor beams (John Prescott MP). And finally the biggest thing of all, which was a moat.

Douglas Hogg, Conservative MP for Sleaford and Hykeham, was also the Third Viscount Hailsham. He had a good record as a minister in John Major's government. His father and grandfather had been cabinet ministers before him, though he told me once that politics was no longer a profession that he would recommend to his own children. He owned a substantial manor house in Lincolnshire and the moat that encircled it. The manor house, of course, was designated as his second home. He had a special deal with the Fees Office, the House of Commons accounts department, to help him with the estate's expenses. These included £2,115 for having his moat cleaned, and further amounts to get his stable lights fixed and his piano tuned; there was also money for a mole man and a call-out charge for someone to deal with the bees. The moat was not specifically claimed for, but not excluded either. Its cleaning caught the imagination of people who did not own moats, stables or even pianos; and who, if they had problems with moles or bees, would pay the cost themselves of getting them fixed. It was the perfect metaphor for the perception of MPs leading privileged lives remote from the rest of us in a world entirely their own. It was also in keeping with the idea of Parliament as a fortress. The symbol of the House of Commons is a portcullis: now we understand why. Mr Hogg, who did not enjoy the adverse publicity, decided to stand down from Parliament and endure no more of it.

The moat immediately became a national talking point. The newly-appointed Poet Laureate, Carol Ann Duffy, laid down a marker with her very first official verse, an off-the-cuff couplet delivered during a visit to a school in Manchester:

What did they do with the trust of your vote?
Hired a flunky to flush out the moat.

It was famous abroad as well as at home. To the Americans especially, it was evidence of the undefeatable daftness and dottiness of the British. But the *New York Times* was faintly disappointed. 'When British politicians go astray,' it sniffed, 'one expects spies or sex. Yet the latest scandal is about Parliament members and their expense accounts.'[4] On Comedy Central's popular evening show, influential in the election of Barack Obama, a British actor put the case for owning a moat to the astonished host, Jon Stewart. Patriotic music played in the background. He struck a heroic pose. It was his Richard II moment.

'You probably never dug a trough around anything you owned and filled it with stagnant water. My country may not defend itself with guns, but we will encircle ourselves with a trough of filthy water. ...

And we will fight for this corrupt plot, this filth, this scam, this England!'

It was a topsy-turvy time, this age of scandal, in which the people took the comedians seriously but saw the politicians as a joke.

By a happy coincidence Garrison Keillor, the sage of Minnesota, was in London at the height of the parliamentary revelations and wrote about them in woebegone wonderment for the *New York Times*: 'And now, having seen the Speaker walk the plank, the Honourables must go out to their districts in Sodden Wickham and Twitching Bridgewater to explain why taxpayers paid for the cleaning of a moat. A dreadful fate, having to kneel down and crawl in public as the mob flings dead fish and dry dog dung at you. ... Forget about Iran – if Mr Obama is charging us for his trouser press, we want to know.'[5]

The Iranian supreme leader Ayatollah Ali Khamenei, singling out Britain for attack after a disputed election, used the scandal as evidence of corruption in Western countries preying on Iran 'like wolves'. The *Zimbabwe Herald*, mouthpiece of Robert Mugabe, suggested that Zimbabwean politicians needed higher salaries lest they be tempted into corrupt practices like British MPs. And politicians in the Turks and Caicos, a dependent territory in the Caribbean, asked how the British dared to suspend their constitution, on grounds of alleged corruption, in the light of what was happening in their own Parliament – and what kind of example was that?

At home it was like the start of the hunting season, with MPs as the quarry. Not just a few, but a substantial number of them – at first 100, then 200, and in the end at least a half – were named and shamed and vilified as never before, at least since the 18th century. There were so many of them that total honesty was seen as an exception. In drawing up lists it saved time to single out the saints rather than the sinners – the frugal minority who had not abused their allowances or claimed second homes when they did not need them. These included Adam Afriyie (Conservative, Windsor), Anne Milton (Conservative, Guildford), Geoffrey Robinson (Labour, Coventry North West), Martin Salter (Labour, Reading West) and David Howarth (Liberal Democrat, Cambridge). Kelvin Hopkins (Labour, Luton North) earned a mention in despatches for having claimed only £4,513 in four years while his neighbour Margaret Moran (Luton South), who lived in the same street, claimed £74,904. It was especially good to see the millionaire Geoffrey Robinson on the saints' list, after his earlier falling out with the Committee on Standards and Privileges. Overall the sinners were a majority, the saints a handful and the rest of the MPs in borderline territory between them.

I had long suspected, from my time on Standards and Privileges, that many MPs were more concerned with their privileges than their standards. This seemed to be confirmed by some of the arithmetic. There was now a league table of MPs' costs, ranging from the bargain basement Philip Hollobone (Conservative, Kettering) to the top-of-the-line, gold-plated and ultra de luxe Eric Joyce (Labour, Falkirk). Tom Levitt, the Labour MP for High Peak, who had served with me on the Committee, was the eighth most expensive Member in that particular pecking order. He had claimed £8,013.77 to refit the bathroom of his London home, and even £16.50 for a Remembrance Day wreath. The wreath was claimed in error, he said. The bathroom was a necessary expense. And he accused the *Telegraph* of conniving in gutter journalism.

It was noted that across the Commons, but chiefly within the two main parties, there was a pattern in all of this state-funded extravagance. The highest claimants of the Alternative Costs Allowance were also the MPs most obedient to the bidding of the whips. There was nothing they wouldn't claim for or, when the division bell sounded, vote for. They would dutifully troop through the lobbies and pocket their tax-free allowances. The independent-minded tended to claim far less. Dennis Skinner was notably frugal. Yet some of the offenders on the Tory side were long-serving Members with reputations, until these scandals broke, as respected and effective constituency MPs. They were also country gentlemen of the old school who lived in considerable style. And theirs were the claims that kept the people talking and the cartoonists working overtime. The *Telegraph*'s Matt was in a particularly rich vein of form. The moat was just the start of it.

Anthony Steen was the Conservative Member for Totnes. He had been a diligent constituency MP since

1983, with a reputation for endearing battiness, which he advertised on his website. He was best known for intervening at Prime Minister's Question Time to invite the occupant of Number Ten to visit his cockle fishers in South Devon. Cockle fishers never had a more devoted champion. In due course he might well have been honoured as a knight of the shires – it used to happen in an MP's sixth term – but events got in the way. I rather liked him. The endearing battiness was genuine. He seemed every inch a character out of Gilbert and Sullivan: so much so that he once persuaded me to initiate a debate on Arts Council funding for the D'Oyly Carte Opera Company. It turned out that the House, from the Speaker on down, had a passion for light opera. Anthony Steen had an office just down the corridor from mine during most of my time as an MP. It was grander, of course, but still just a single room in Dean's Yard near Westminster Abbey. He lived in greater style in his constituency. Over four years he claimed £87,729 to maintain this country house as his second home. The costs included money to inspect 500 trees and to guard his shrubs from rabbits. He was an MP after all. And it would never do for an Honourable Member's trees to fall down or his estate to be overrun by rabbits.

But his arrangements, when they became known, were anathema to his party's leadership. David Cameron demanded that he stand down at the next election, which he duly agreed to do. He then gave a most extraordinary interview to the BBC which suggested that compliance was one thing but repentance was another. 'I have done nothing criminal,' he said, 'and you know what it's about? Jealousy. I have got a very, very large house. Some people say it looks like Balmoral, but it's a merchant's house from the 19th century. ... You know what this reminds me of? An episode of *Coronation Street*. This is a kangaroo court.' He was then required to apologise and to remain silent on the issue, upon pain of expulsion from the party. The Conservatives were striving to shed their patrician image, and the exposure of the Toff of Totnes did not suit their electoral strategy.

Nor did the expenses of Sir John Butterfill, whose modest flat in his Bournemouth constituency was claimed as his main home. That left him free to designate as his second home, partly funded by the taxpayer, a six-bedroom mansion near Woking. The taxpayers' subsidy for this included £17,000 for servants' quarters, for grandees need servants much as ducks need ponds; and we shall arrive at the duck pond shortly. Sir John eventually sold the big house for a profit of £600,000. But by then he declared it to the Revenue as his main home, which was a common practice among MPs, so it was not liable to capital gains tax. Among the many instances of flipping and switching this was the one that, when exposed, required the greatest payback, of £60,000, to the taxman. David Cameron was not amused by these arrangements. 'The lack of common sense and reasonableness has been shocking,' he said. They suggested that his lot were at it as much as the other lot; and that his rebranding of the party still had some way to go.

The case of Sir Peter Viggers was an even greater embarrassment to the Tories and gift to the cartoonists. Sir Peter was the long-serving MP for Gosport in Hampshire. I had known him in the Commons as an eloquent champion of the military hospitals, which were threatened and eventually closed by successive governments just when the armed services most sorely needed them. But the naval hospital in his constituency was not his only water-related interest. He had also claimed £1,645 for a 'pond feature' which turned out to be a floating duck island on his Hampshire estate. It was a considerable construction, this duck island: a five-foot edifice designed on the lines of an 18th-century mansion in Stockholm. The ducks never had it so grand. The Fees Office, in a rare display of austerity, had actually refused to pay for it. But the duck island replaced the moat as the most striking symbol of parliamentary excess.

'What the hell's a duck island?' asked an exasperated David Cameron. And Sir Peter too was required to stand down at the next election.

At this point, because it was a British revolution, the British press went quackers. Never mind the more serious cases of outright fraud and embezzlement: as far as the headlines were concerned it was the trivia that took wing and did the damage. There were features about duck farms, duck islands, duck houses and every recorded species of the bird: mallards, teals, mandarins, shovelers and 158 other varieties. Experts were found who questioned the usefulness of duck houses or islands as a protection against foxes; it turned out that foxes could swim. And when all this became known, Sir Peter admitted not only that he was ashamed and humiliated by the episode, 'a ridiculous and grave error of judgement', but that the ducks had not taken to their new home either. So he had sent it away to another of his properties, which was a chateau in France. Later he decided to sell it for charity – and probably for a high price too, since it was by then the world's most famous duck island.

He was born after his time. In the reign of Charles II he would have been a strong candidate for the well-paid post of Governor of the King's Ducks.

Next up for inspection was Parliament's Mr Clean. This was the title awarded to Mike Hall, the Labour MP for Weaver Vale in Cheshire, which is the town of Northwich and some of its outlying districts. His second home was a small house in Kensington. In three years he spent nearly £15,000 of taxpayers' money on keeping it and his clothes clean. In 2005/6 he claimed £5,194 for his cleaning bills; in 2006/7 this went down to £4,346, before going back up again in 2007/8 to £5,408. The Fees Office, to its credit, asked him for details and he then came up with the goods: 'Cleaning cloths, sponges, kitchen towels, toilet tissue, floor kitchen window and oven cleaning fluids, bathroom cleaners, disinfectant, bleach, laundry products, stain removers, air fresheners, polish, bin-bags and vermin and pest sprays.'

Surely there was never a more spotless MP than the Member for Weaver Vale. People then asked me quite reasonably, since I was presumed to have a high laundry bill, who had paid for the dry-cleaning of the white suits while I was MP for Tatton (which happened to include the other parts of Northwich: Mr Hall and I had a somewhat strained relationship). I took them to Johnson's in Princess Street, Knutsford, and I paid the bills myself. Nor did I charge for bleach, polish, disinfectant or any other cleaning agent. It never occurred to me that such routine and everyday expenses could be laid at the door of the ever-generous taxpayer. Nor did anyone tell me about the 'John Lewis list' which set the limits on allowable expenses. Oh, the plasma TVs and fitted kitchens that I could have claimed! Or the second homes I could have switched! Seen in this light, I realise now that I never knew a flipping thing; and that my political career was a catalogue of missed opportunities. After it was over, I worked out that if I had pushed every allowance to the limit I could have made an extra £62,000 tax-free over the four years. But it would not have looked too good if it had all come out, so to speak, in the wash. My successor in Tatton, George Osborne (£440 for a taxi from Tatton to London), once unkindly called me the dry cleaners' candidate.

Besides, it was too late now to write to the Fees Office and seek reimbursement for the £15 I had spent on a hanging basket in June 2000 in the village of Mere near Knutsford. It was in a double sense a mere £15, but a beautiful hanging basket. It adorned my cottage in Church Street, Great Budworth for a whole summer. When I was away, it was watered by a very kind man across the road with family connections to Neil

Hamilton: it was thus a bipartisan hanging basket, the symbol of the flowering of new politics. Its colours were red, blue, yellow, white and purple. Whatever the party or non-party, the hanging basket had a bloom for it. So now, in looking back on it with the claims of others in mind, I realise that I had no need to pay for it myself. It was a legitimate expense incurred in the performance of my parliamentary duties. It deserved a mention in *Hansard*. Did Margaret Beckett's hanging baskets deserve a mention in *Hansard*? I somehow doubt it. So the £15 should have been repaid by the Fees Office, but never was, because I did not suppose it was allowable. It was one of the many might-have-beens in a short political career. 'Of all sad words of tongue or pen ...'

Then there was the Garden Man. If the MP for Weaver Vale had the cleanest house, his Honourable Friend the MP for Mansfield may have owned the tidiest garden. Over four years Alan Meale claimed more than £13,000 for his gardening expenses. These included £2,000 for a horticulturalist to clear trees and shrubs from the grounds of his Nottinghamshire home, more money for the repair of footpaths and walls, £69 for garden tools and £188 for topsoil. Since he was a former environment minister, it might have been argued that his gardening interests were entirely appropriate. That would be for the voters to decide. And in 2008 they had already rejected him when he stood as Labour candidate against the popular Independent Mayor of Mansfield, Tony Egginton. Mr Egginton won easily.

The challenge for the political parties was how they would deal, not only with their front-benchers and high spenders, but with middle-of-the-range cases of back-benchers little known outside their constituencies whose use of the Alternative Costs Allowance had, at the very least, generated some local controversy. In the great scheme of things, Mike Hall's cleaning bills and Alan Meale's gardening bills attracted little scrutiny beyond that of their local papers and political opponents. They were unlikely to have to explain themselves before their party's Star Chamber, which was considering some of the more serious cases bordering on fraud. In normal times that would be the end of the matter. They would both be in line to be re-selected and re-elected, if they wished to serve for a further term. But these were not normal times. They might well face Independent challenges from disaffected constituents. In Weaver Vale a well-respected Independent, Mike Cooksley, had already challenged Mike Hall once before, and I was trying to persuade him to do so again to give the MP a run for his cleaning money. Mansfield had previously been more or less a one-party state. Even before they knew about the expenses, its people had already risen up twice in successful rebellions against the Labour establishment. The circumstances favoured a further insurrection. In August 2009 Tony Egginton and his Independents launched a campaign to rusticate the Garden Man, if he were to decide to seek re-election. Their candidate, André Camilleri, said: 'I promise you, if I am elected, Parliament will never be the same again!'

This was a blend of the old politics and the new. New players were announcing their entrances even as old ones were, just possibly, planning their exits. Labour MPs on their way out of the door tended to be slow to give notice of their retirements for a variety of reasons: to wrong-foot their opponents, to make it easier for their party to impose a successor, or not to be seen to be driven out of office by newspaper headlines. Politics would still be politics, whether practised by the political parties or by none-of-the-above Independents. But it would be done in an entirely new climate.

Chapter 2

Accidents Waiting to Happen

We should have seen it coming. A very few did. The squalls of scandal in the late 1980s and early 1990s were a prelude to the great storm of 2009. The sleaze of the Tory years, both real and perceived, was serious enough to bring down a government at a time of economic prosperity and usher in a new one on a pledge to clean up politics. They did not promise to be whiter than white, but they did say purer than pure. We now know it was a hollow promise, but we wished to believe it then. The Tory years were by no means an age of innocence. But most of the two dozen MPs facing accusations of using their public office for private gain were backbenchers and relatively minor figures. Few were senior members of the party. Some resigned and others were defeated. It was a thorough spring cleaning. None of them remained in Parliament. We congratulated ourselves that the system had worked – or, where it hadn't, that the people had finished the job themselves – and we set about strengthening the safeguards against the few rotten apples in the barrel (a favourite term used by defenders of status quo politics to argue that our politicians were, but for a handful, honest and admirable tribunes of the people; we would find out about that in due course).

The new system was a sort of double entrenchment, with one set of defences outside Parliament, the Committee on Standards in Public Life, and another inside Parliament, a Commissioner for Standards reporting to the Committee on Standards and Privileges. These guardians of honest politics would, so it was thought at the time – oh happy days, oh brave new world! – restore public trust in public life, and give us at last a Parliament to be proud of. What was unimaginable was that in the course of a dozen years our level of trust would not only fail to rise significantly, but would fall off the scale altogether.

The external safeguard was the Committee on Standards in Public Life, set up in 1994 after the cash-for-questions affair involving Tim Smith and Neil Hamilton. Under the chairmanship of Lord Nolan, the Committee in its first report set out the seven principles of public life that all MPs were obliged to sign on to. They were honesty, integrity, openness, objectivity, leadership, accountability and selflessness. We were even given them on a little wallet-sized card to remind us of them, just in case we had forgotten what they were. They were a sort of ethical credit card. But many did choose to forget. As the journalist Peter Oborne said in his evidence to the Committee, now under the chairmanship of Sir Christopher Kelly: 'We have had the opposite ever since: dishonesty, secrecy, grotesque lack of leadership on ethical matters, partiality.'[1] Sir Christopher himself observed rather drily that if more MPs had observed the seven principles over the past few years, 'We would not now be where we are.' The sins were individual but the guilt was collective and occasionally admitted. 'I confess we are all responsible for this', said the Justice Secretary Jack Straw.[2]

When the details of MPs' expenses finally came out, there turned out to be almost as many dodgy schemes as dodgy Members. Each case was different but all had one thing in common. The MPs involved, even if they had acted within the elastic rules that they set themselves, were clearly in breach of the seven principles of public life. Where was the honesty in flipping homes? Where was the integrity in charging for mole traps? Where was the leadership in billing the taxpayer for a Remembrance Day wreath? Where was the selflessness in pushing every allowance to the limit of what they could get away with? And when, in the midst of it all, Gordon Brown proposed a new code of conduct for MPs, it was never actually implemented because there was no need for it. The code of conduct already existed. All that was necessary was to replace MPs who would not observe it with MPs who would.

The problem that the Committee had, under a succession of chairmen, was that the government, and especially the Prime Minister, took very little notice of it. This was especially true of a Prime Minister, Tony Blair, who had been elected in 1997 at 'a time of hope beyond ordinary imagining' (his phrase for it) on a promise to clean up politics. Sir Alistair Graham, the Committee's chairman from 2004 to 2007, was especially outspoken and therefore especially sidelined. In May 2006 he accused Tony Blair of 'a major error of judgement' on issues of ethical standards: 'He has paid a heavy price for ignoring standards. We would have preferred more positive support from the Prime Minister. We suspect he is pretty lukewarm towards what we do.'[3] Sir Alistair's reward was to be let go at the earliest opportunity. In his departing speech in 2007 he said: 'My greatest regret has been the apparent failure to persuade the government to place high ethical standards at the heart of its thinking and, more importantly, behaviour.'[4] So we had plenty of warning. The position of chairman was then left unfilled for the next eight months, while the Committee was parked and virtually out of action. There were those in government who regarded it as a bit of a nuisance.

The internal safeguard was the Parliamentary Commissioner for Standards, who would examine complaints against MPs and report to the Committee on Standards and Privileges. The first Commissioner was Sir Gordon Downey, a distinguished servant of the House of Commons; he took it on reluctantly and found it a bruising experience. It was he who decided there was 'compelling evidence' that the MP for Tatton, Neil Hamilton, had received £20,000 in cash in brown envelopes from the owner of Harrods, Mohammed al Fayed. I mention this now not to settle old scores but because, as the expenses scandal unfolded, some people wondered, hadn't Neil Hamilton been harshly treated for an unproven misdemeanour? His name was occasionally mentioned as someone who had perhaps been wronged by the system. A constituent of one of the many exposed MPs observed: 'Compared to what she has done, the Hamiltons were saints.' It is worth recalling therefore that Hamilton sued al Fayed for libel in 1999. At the end of the trial George Carman, in his last case, showed that Hamilton had tabled an amendment to Clause 116 of the Finance Bill in 1989 which, if it had been passed, would have saved the oil industry £70 million in taxes. He then invoiced Mobil for £10,000 for his parliamentary services. 'He was actually trying to change the law,' said Mr Carman, 'and seeking payment for that work.' In terms of the scandals of 2009, that would put him at somewhere about the middle order of disgraced MPs. Just because today's MPs were guilty, it did not follow that yesterday's were guiltless. The jury found Mohammed al Fayed a more credible witness than Neil Hamilton. That spoke for itself.

As for the workings of the Committee on Standards and Privileges, they were not as free from party politics as they should have been. I served on the Committee from December 1997 to May 2001. It was a difficult time, because both the two main parties politicised the new system by using it to try to discredit each other in a series of tit-for-tat sleaze allegations. In February 1998 Sir Gordon Downey was succeeded by Elizabeth Filkin as the Commissioner. She had formerly been Adjudicator of the Inland Revenue, which is one of the toughest jobs in public service; but nothing prepared her for the obstruction and ill-will that she met as Commissioner for Standards. It was clear from the outset that her zeal disturbed some of the Labour MPs on the Committee and those whom they defended in the House. I do not know to this day if they were taking instructions from the whips, but their actions were consistent with some kind of outside influence. They could not have decided as they did on the evidence contained in the piles of papers that we hauled into the Committee room. One of them tried to influence a decision by remote control even in his absence from a crucial Committee meeting. The case that caused the greatest difficulty, dragging on for nearly a year, was a complaint against Dr John Reid, the government's enforcer and man for all ministries (£199 for a pouffe), for allegedly misusing his parliamentary allowances. Although he personally was no doubt blameless, his friends initiated a whispering campaign that swirled from the tea room to the Speaker's office, and led eventually to the downfall of Elizabeth Filkin. She upheld an important part of the complaint against him. The Committee, which was divided but worked by consensus, did not. I was in the minority and with the Commissioner and two others. I should have resigned from it then and there, but did not. It was my greatest mistake as an MP.

Consistently throughout these years, none of the checks on MPs' conduct worked. At the heart of the problem was a lack of transparency and external scrutiny. None of the parliamentary defences put in place by the reforms of 1994 prevented MPs plundering the Exchequer. They could do as they wished within reason and beyond it. The expenses system was out of control. There was no independent audit. The culture was pernicious. The House of Commons behaved like a company that certified its own accounts or hired a hole-in-the-wall firm of book-keepers, good friends of the chairman, to sign off on them. It was the political equivalent of Kenneth Lay's Enron or Bernie Madoff's Madoff Investments. Like them the House was a self-certifying institution. Its Fees Office was treated like a cash machine. The money was available and the Honourable Members made off with it.

Many regarded it as only their due – a common argument that embezzlers make to themselves – since they were only making up in allowances what they had been denied in salary. For more than twenty years MPs' pay had been held down for fear of the popular backlash if they voted themselves anything more than a modest rise. Harry Cohen, Labour MP for Leyton and Wanstead, was candid about it. He named as his main home a holiday caravan in Mersea so that his second home could be his house in the constituency. Over the years he claimed more than £300,000 on expenses on this house. He described it as part of his salary in all but name – 'That is what it exists for.' The practice had begun under Margaret Thatcher, when she was trying to head off a rebellion by some of her backbenchers about how little they were paid. According to Harry Cohen, one of her

ministers, John Moore, said: 'Go out boys and spend it.'[5]
And so they did. For had they not earned it? A complaint
against Mr Cohen was referred to the Parliamentary
Commissioner for Standards. Mr Cohen objected to the
'incessant intrusion' into the life of his family and, like
so many others, in June 2009 he decided to stand down.

New Labour had not only failed to crack down on
the allowances, but had actually increased them. It had
introduced a communications allowance to help MPs
keep in touch with their constituents. The theory was
that the local papers no longer reported their achieve-
ments with the prominence they deserved, so they would
do it for themselves – all, naturally, at the taxpayers'
expense. That was the way it worked. MPs could adver-
tise themselves freely. Party propaganda was funded by
public money.

This obviously favoured incumbents over challeng-
ers, and the Labour Party over the other parties, since
Labour had the largest number of MPs. But it was about
to backfire. For in the midst of the expenses scandal,
being an incumbent was suddenly not an advantage after
all. MPs had expected to run on their records, but more
on their voting records than their gardening and cleaning bills. All the communications allowances in the world
could not repair the damage of how much they had actually claimed at the public expense.

There were some who reproached me for having
been instrumental in the Conservatives' downfall but
then having turned a blind eye to the scandals of the
Labour years. And it is true that, like everyone else,

I had little idea of the extent of the corruption that would later be revealed. But I was concerned enough in 2007 to write a book about it. It started with the Bernie Ecclestone case, in which the Formula 1 magnate had given a million pounds to the Labour Party which then changed its policy on tobacco advertising in a way that, quite by chance, suited his business interests. It laid out the details of improprieties that were then in the public domain, involving not just backbenchers but cabinet ministers, some of whom – Peter Mandelson, John Prescott and David Blunkett to name but three – were identified as repeat offenders. It argued that self-regulation did not and would not work. It called for a tougher disciplinary system than the one that was then in place. It didn't mince words: it described the rising political class as a collection of creeps, cranks and careerists. It concluded: 'We have reached a point where the scope for improvement, in the conduct and reputation of MPs, is surely much greater than at any time since 1832.'[6] The book was published in 2007 and of course came under fire from friends of the creeps, cranks and careerists. Joe Haines, a Downing Street veteran from Harold Wilson's days, said it showed that journalists should not be MPs. What it actually showed was that many of the present gang should not be MPs either. If I had known then what I know now, it would have been harsher and larger: three volumes would hardly do justice to the scale of the scandal.

Because I was elected to the Commons on an issue of trust, I had to be very careful about expenses. It was a matter of common sense as much as principle. I had no genial old-timer to put his hand on my shoulder – as certainly used to happen to new reporters in the old newsrooms – to explain what could be claimed within the letter of the rules, and to urge me not to spoil it for everyone else. No one told me not to rock the boat. Instead, I was presented with a hard-backed green folder on the allowances, which were further explained by a courteous Fees Office clerk. So the alibi of ignorance was not available, to me or to anyone else. But the rules themselves were generous even then. Every month I was invited to sign two cheques to myself. One was for accommodation: my little cottage in Great Budworth near Northwich cost me £7,000 a year in rent, but I could have claimed up to £12,000 without batting an eyelid or producing a single piece of documentary evidence; all the profit would have been tax-free. The other was for mileage within the constituency: and most MPs, even some in big cities, claimed up to the maximum of some 400 miles a month; it took no more than an honourable signature at the foot of the page. Some MPs from the North East were known to share a car to travel up from London on Thursday afternoons and back on Monday mornings. These journeys were then billed for individually to the Members' financial advantage. If the money was there to be taken, then they took it – much like those journalists of the old school whose expense accounts (like a few of their reports) were magnificent works of fiction. I knew an American TV correspondent who billed his company for moving his junk from

Hong Kong to Los Angeles; and then, because it was a real junk, he sailed it there. The only difference was that the MPs, unlike the reporters, couldn't play the black market in dodgy foreign currencies. Since then the news organisations, like all companies, had tightened their procedures to allow only modest expenses against receipts. In the House of Commons alone did the lobbies and corridors lead to a pot of gold.

Part of the problem was the disease of *Westminsteritis* – that sense of entitlement that comes with being a big shot in the community. I looked in the mirror and saw it in myself. MPs become proprietary about the places they represent, and take a reasonable pride in them, even if they are only there for a single term. They are tempted to see themselves as the chief citizens of their constituencies. They are VIPs with a mandate. Whether they care to take it or not, they have a place of honour at the mayor-making, the May Day ceremony, the Remembrance Day parade, the charity ball, the flower show, the gooseberry festival, the ploughing match, the Christmas pantomime, the fire brigade open day, the high school prize-giving and all the other public events in the calendar. Even local councillors of other parties will (usually) treat them with a measure of respect. They expect their press releases to be published verbatim as gospel in the local papers. They make speeches and unveil plaques. (Occasionally, if they fall into disgrace – and I have seen this happen – the plaques are discreetly and quietly removed.) They put themselves about. They set an example, in their own eyes at least, of devoted public service. They are – or at least they used to be, until the present upheavals – looked up to for the qualities that they see in themselves. So they expect this deference to be matched at Westminster, if not in their relationship with other MPs, who also have their own strong sense of entitlement, at least in their dealings with the lower orders in parliamentary departments like the Fees Office. The Commons accountants, like all the servants of the House, are certainly not seen as equals, but subtly looked down on, and regarded as a potential nuisance which has to be squared away or kept in its box. During this disastrous period they were left in the invidious position of checking on their employers' expenses and enquiring whether a claim for reimbursement – £398.95 for a sat nav system in a rural constituency (David Jones, Conservative, Clwyd West), or £29.99 for a black glitter toilet seat (Dr John Reid, Labour, Airdrie and Shotts) – was within the rules. It would not be surprising if some had nervous breakdowns, or if one of them was sufficiently upset to blow the whistle on the whole conspiracy.

The relationship between the MPs and their accountants was too close for comfort, including a degree of unwitting or unwilling complicity. Sir Philip Mawer, Elizabeth Filkin's successor as Parliamentary Commissioner for Standards, testified to the Kelly Committee on Standards in Public Life that MPs had been told that what they would not be given through the front door, in terms of increases in pay, they would be given through the back door, in terms of the allowances system. A sort of creeping collusion occurred between the Members and the Fees Office: 'At one time it has been said to me the duty of staff was to enable Members to claim the maximum, not to police the allowances system.'[7] That is the time-honoured way with corruption. It does not arrive and announce itself with a flourish. It seeps in under the door.

MPs' correspondence with the Fees Office, which they never imagined would see the light of day, is wonderfully revealing about the almost feudal nature of their relationship. Sir Gerald Kaufman MP (Labour, Manchester Gorton), who claimed for a £1,851 rug and £8,865 for a TV set, wrote to a Fees Office official: 'Why are you querying these expenses?' And on another occasion he threatened to make a complaint unless a dispute was settled by noon the following day.

In 2006 a Commons official wrote to Margaret Beckett, querying one of her claims for repairs to her second home in her Derby constituency. She wrote: 'We live in an old cottage, not the beautiful, strong stone-built type, but the kind of thing you throw together for the farm workers from the bricks you had when you knocked down the pigsty – and it requires a good deal of maintenance and repair.' It also required garden plants and hanging baskets – £1,380-worth of them over a period of three years. She may well have come to regret those hanging baskets.

Sir Alan Haselhurst, the Conservative MP for Saffron Walden who twice aspired to the Speakership, was one of many who did not appreciate being asked by officials in the Fees Office for documentary evidence to support his claims. In March 2006 he sent a message to his questioners: 'I can't understand why you are doing this to me, you have paid me the last eleven months without querying my claims, I want you to call me back today with an answer.' He later acknowledged public concerns about MPs' expenses; and in May 2009 he announced that he would pay back £12,000 in gardening costs 'out of respect to my constituents'.

The Fees Office gave no public account of its stewardship. One of its former staff recalled having sought to challenge an MP about one of his expense claims. He was stopped in his tracks not by the MP but by one of his seniors in the office. 'You have to understand,' said the official, 'that we are dealing here with *Honourable Members*.'

Dr Tony Wright MP, chairman of the Public Administration Committee, had been warning of the expenses apocalypse for seven years, when he gave evidence to the Committee on Standards in Public Life, then chaired by Sir Nigel Wicks, in the wake of the assisted departure of Elizabeth Filkin. He told them that the next scandal would be about MPs' expenses, and the time to do something about it was now. That was in 2002. 'When I said what I did,' he remarked, 'it was not an unusual prescience on my part, it was just a statement of the blindingly obvious. Here was a problem and, if it was not attended to, it was going to cause us grief. It was not attended to. Why was it not attended to? Because people had a great interest in not having it attended to. ... Right up to the end, until the sky really did fall in, people thought perhaps they could find a way around it.'[8]

While the *Telegraph* got the scoop, and the boost in circulation that went with it, much of the credit belonged to Heather Brooke, a determined Anglo-American journalist who was a self-taught expert on the Freedom of Information Act. The Act was passed in 2000 and had a long gestation period: it did not come into effect until January 2005. By then she had written a book, *The Freedom of Information Act: a Citizen's Right to Know*. From October 2004 she started to press for information about MPs' travel expenses, their second home allowances, and the employment of their families. She was looking for the same transparency in Westminster that she had found in Washington. She was disappointed. Her requests were resisted by the House and especially by its Commission and its Speaker, Michael Martin. She was threatened with bankruptcy. She and two other journalists, Ben Leapman of the *Sunday Telegraph* and Jon Ungoed-Thomas of the *Sunday Times*, appealed to the Information Commissioner, Richard Thomas, who ordered the release of information about ten selected MPs. This provoked an intense rearguard action by the House authorities. The journalists prevailed in the High Court. The judges ruled: 'We are not here dealing with idle gossip, or public curiosity about what in truth are trivialities. The expenditure of public money through the payment of MPs' salaries and allowances is a matter of direct and reasonable interest to taxpayers.'

With typical modesty, Heather Brooke downplayed her role in bringing the scandal to light. She gave the credit, if that was the right word for it, to the House of Commons authorities themselves. 'I do not really feel that I have done that much,' she said, 'really it was the Speaker and the officials of the House of Commons that did most to make this story and to have such sort of catastrophic results.'[9] Some of these officials were later rewarded with considerable salary increases.

Public opinion also had a major impact. In April 2007 David Maclean (Conservative, Penrith and The Border), proposed a Private Member's Bill that would have exempted the Houses of Parliament from the Freedom of Information Act. He was a former Conservative Chief Whip who was one of three backbenchers in the magic circle of the leadership – the House of Commons Commission which, on matters of pay and allowances, becomes the Members Estimate Committee. The other two were Nick Harvey MP (Liberal Democrat) and Sir Stuart Bell (Labour). They played an important part, backstage, in the saga of MPs' expenses. The reformers tended to view them, without admiration, as the vanguard of the rearguard.

David Maclean had a reputation, together with his friend the late Eric Forth MP, for torpedoing Members' Private Bills, other than his own, on grounds of cost. They played for time and were masters of the filibuster. They were like a football team forever back-passing and playing for a draw. Their time-wasting upset me so much that I challenged them once on the floor of the House, to ask them what was the point of it, and of course got nowhere. They were professionals who had been in the House for years and whose mastery of parliamentary procedure was of course much greater than mine. Mr Maclean's Freedom of Information (Amendment) Bill was fast-tracked through the Commons despite the opposition of principled rebels like Mark Fisher (Labour), Richard Shepherd (Conservative) and Norman Baker (Liberal Democrat), who warned that no good would come of it. Mr Maclean said: 'My Bill is necessary to give an absolute guarantee that the correspondence of Members of Parliament, on behalf of their constituents and others, to a public authority remains confidential.'[10] The Bill would also have kept MPs' expenses secret, including his own, which were not at the low end of the scale – though to be fair, because of failing health, he needed some special provision. Ninety-eight MPs, including twenty ministers, voted for the Bill. According to one of the rebels, this was a gauche attempt to circumvent the Freedom of Information Act, and suggested a high degree of complicity between government ministers, the whips and the House of Commons authorities. It showed the House of Commons at its worst.

Their campaign failed. So great was the outcry against Mr Maclean's Bill that not a single peer could be found to sponsor it in the Lords; and so it never reached the statute book. That was quite an achievement in Parliament – a Bill so disreputable that no one would support it. Even the usual suspects and stooges had gone to ground on this one, which in a crowded field was a welcome surprise. The rebels hailed the outcome as a triumph of democracy over the self-interest of politicians. Because the day of reckoning was approaching, a last-ditch stand was made by the Leader of the House, Harriet Harman, in January 2009. Labour MPs were put under a three-line whip to back it – and, knowing what we know now, it is easy to understand why they were so anxious to keep their personal records, and those of others, from public view. Even then it was clear that they must have had something to hide. The opposition parties rebelled, the measure was dropped, and the way was open for the whole shocking story to be told. This happened within a matter of weeks; and of course the House gave up its secrets despite itself and not out of any belief in openness and transparency.

The origin of the revelations, through some mysterious back channel, was the Fees Office. There was a mole in there somewhere, and not the sort that MPs sought the taxpayers' help to deal with. In an earlier age a scandal on this scale would have been less likely, if only because it would have been difficult to walk away with the thousands of pages on which the records were kept. But the IT revolution was the MPs' undoing. Somewhere and somehow the damning details were copied onto computer disks, which were subsequently auctioned to the press and acquired by the *Daily Telegraph*. It was an untidy process, and in the course of it some of the early details, for instance on Jacqui Smith's financial arrangements, appeared in other newspapers before the deal was sealed. The fee was reported to be in the region of

£70,000, which would make it a bargain in the annals of cheque-book journalism. The ex-wives of celebrities and disgraced MPs get that for a single interview. Scotland Yard was asked by the House of Commons Commission to investigate the 'theft' of the MPs' files but wisely declined to do so. It was not theft at all. It was a public service.

The middleman was John Wick, a former soldier of the SAS and the Parachute Regiment, who headed a security company. Although he was presumed to have benefited financially, he also set aside his Conservative sympathies and claimed to have acted in the public interest. 'This was a scandal across the political spectrum,' he said, 'with some Conservative MPs' behaviour as reprehensible as their Labour counterparts'. The public release of the information had to be thorough, across every party, and the Conservatives would have to accept the consequences with the other parties.'[11] It was part of the general pattern, however, that although both main parties were heavily implicated, the Conservatives' abuses of the system inclined towards the comical and the Labour abuses, in certain cases, towards the edge of the criminal. On one side stood the moats and duck islands, and on the other the phantom mortgages.

Another intermediary was identified as Henry Gewanter, a PR consultant who had acted, he said, without a fee in placing the 'scoop of the century' (his term for it) in the *Telegraph*. 'I thought it would be a very simple, straightforward job,' he said, 'but to my surprise it turned out to be one of the most difficult, complicated and long-running projects of my entire life.' The negotiations with various newspapers involved protection of the source and the use to which the information would be put. It would have been all too easy to go down the road of party propaganda. 'One of the prime conditions was that whichever newspaper did get the exclusive had to be willing to cover every MP who misbehaved from whatever party. There is at least one newspaper who wanted to use it to destroy one party.'[12]

The *Telegraph* received its windfall at a time when, to outside observers of the newspaper scene, it seemed to be in a state of permanent turbulence. Its loyal readers were predominantly elderly, and even by making successive changes to the format and look of the paper, it had not succeeded in adding to their dwindling ranks. For all the pretty girls on the masthead it remained essentially a settled, establishment paper. If it moved too fast it would shed old readers without acquiring new ones. It had invested heavily in an online edition, including even a TV service of uneven quality, but like its competitors had not yet found a way of making money from the internet. Morale was not high. Budget cuts had depleted its editorial ranks, and some able foreign correspondents had been culled for what seemed to many of us to be no good reason. We had friends on the paper; many of them were disaffected, and we speculated that, for a while at least, the editorial power to hire and fire had been left in the wrong hands.

Certainly if one visited the *Telegraph*'s much vaunted state-of-the-art hub-and-spoke headquarters in Victoria, as I did at an early stage of the scandal, it seemed to lack the buzz of a busy newsroom. Before computers colonised them, newsrooms used to be great clattering, bustling, noisy places; now they have the hush of a cathedral. The staff cuts had also taken their toll. At what should have been an active time in the news day, I counted twice as many desks as journalists. But there was a hidden reason for this. The paper's 45-strong expenses team – reporters, researchers and editors – had been locked away in a secure area known as The Bunker. There they pored over the million documents that they had acquired – letters, expense forms, bills, receipts and exchanges between the MPs and the Fees Office. Not all the evidence was in their hands: mortgage claims, for instance, had to be checked with the Land Registry. It was slow, painstaking work; and it was this, rather than a wish to stretch out the scoop for as long as possible, that kept the story running for as long as it did.

The paper was also fortunate in having in Ben Brogan, newly recruited from the *Daily Mail*, a political commentator who understood from the start that the force was with the quiet revolutionaries. Ben Brogan knew what was going on. He predicted that, with deselections, retirements and defeats, as many as half the present Members of the House could be shown the door by their parties, or by the voters. He wrote: 'No wonder that the Tory back benches are seething: it is dawning on them that they are being culled.'[13] Although the *Telegraph* is a Tory paper and its opening salvo was directed against Labour cabinet ministers, it did not spare the Conservatives' blushes or present its findings in a partisan way. Abuses of the allowances system were as widespread among Tory as among Labour MPs, and in some cases even more spectacular. In salute to Sir Peter Viggers of duck island fame, the *Telegraph*'s complete expenses file, published as a 68-page supplement on 20 June 2009, was adorned by a solitary duck on its front cover.

Without its scoop, few if any of the most serious individual scandals would have come to light. The worst abuses were systematically – and I would say cynically – wiped from the versions of MPs' expenses later put online by the House itself. It was thanks to the *Telegraph* that the full facts were known and the people's insurrection achieved the force and focus that it did. Its editor Will Lewis had a once-in-an-editorship chance, and took it. If he had been a soldier – and the *Telegraph* was still the officers' newspaper – he should have earned the DSO, a commander's decoration for steadiness under fire. His paper could be forgiven for congratulating itself. It had profited commercially, selling on average an extra 19,000 copies a day. But it had also done the nation and the House of Commons a public service. It knew that the impact would be permanent: 'This is the first time that such detailed information about our elected representatives has been available in one place. It is an historic moment. We believe that the *Daily Telegraph* Expenses Files will help change the face of British politics for ever.'[14]

And so they did.

Chapter 3

The Backlash

The day after the MPs' expenses scandal broke I was on my way to Somalia for UNICEF. For most of the next week I was visiting refugee camps, community centres and government offices in the semi-autonomous province of Puntland, famous for its pirates who had extracted $150 million in ransom from shipping lines in 2008 alone: a UN official who had seen the satellite imagery described the hijacked freighters off the fishing village of Eyl as being parked like limos outside a five-star hotel. The pirates' prosperity was inflating even the Nairobi property market. At the same time the capital, Mogadishu, was under attack by a heavily armed force of 4,000 rebels including 2,000 foreign fighters, Pakistanis, Afghans, Chechens and even some 'brothers in Islam' of European appearance. They came very close to a successful military coup. One of their first actions, in the areas of the city that they had taken, was to set up four training schools to turn young Somalis who were little more than schoolboys into holy warriors. One of their teaching tools was a 45-minute videotape made in Pakistan and offering a crash course in everything from ideology to weapons handling. Somalia was becoming even more of a threat than Afghanistan. The jihadists were opening a new front.

This, I thought, might put the little local difficulties of our MPs in some sort of perspective. But it did not. For from a British perspective Somalia was another planet; and when I got home I discovered the true scale of the scandals and of the public response to them, as they had cascaded day after day across the pages of the *Telegraph*. They revealed what I had long suspected, that petty and not-so-petty fraud in the House of Commons was not particular and occasional but pervasive and widespread. Our home-grown pirates were not at sea (to be a sea-faring pirate at least requires some courage). They were to be found among the political class. And their mother ship was the Palace of Westminster.

I have never known a time when everyone was talking so much of politics and politicians, their expenses and how much they cost. Most of the MPs were slow to understand the strength and depth of the national uprising against them. It passed beyond disgruntlement into rebellion. The voters wondered, when would they get it? Some of them never did. They were publicly contrite but privately defiant, as if they were the victims and not the culprits. Their initial response, that what they had done was within the rules, enraged us even more. For who made the rules? They did. Who policed the rules? They did. And when the rules were broken, who decided on penalties? They did that too. The great debate on the issue of the day was not between one set of politicians and another. It was between the political class and the people. We were all caught up in it. And that was as it should have been, because the perception of corruption was not got up by the press. (The regional press at the time was extremely weak, as newspapers closed their front offices or folded completely.) There was no outside agency or interest fomenting public opinion. It began and ended with the politicians themselves. We did not do this to them. They did it to themselves. Nor was it the effect of any particular voting system, although ours is notoriously defective. It was the effect of having too many creepy and self-serving MPs all present and recumbent, mostly in safe seats, under a system that allowed them to loot the public purse; and to have done so for more years than we knew.

The decline was steep and the fall was painful. As recently as 2002 the chairman of the Lobby journalists with access to Number Ten, James Hardy, had told the Committee on Standards in Public Life: 'People do not generally think there is a problem with corruption in the House of Commons.'[1] By 2009 the popular opinion of MPs had changed completely, from a general perception of honesty to one of dishonesty. A YouGov poll in the *Telegraph* in February 2008 showed that a startling 79 per cent agreed with the statement: 'Most MPs use public office to make money improperly.' And that was before their expenses were exposed in lurid detail. A BBC-commissioned poll confirmed the extent of the voters' hostility: 48 per cent believed that half of all the 646 MPs were actually corrupt. This was a degree of distrust of politicians not known in any other European democracy. It found expression in great tides of anger flowing into the blogosphere, the letters columns of newspapers and radio and television talk shows.

On the day of my return from Somalia, the audience of the BBC's *Question Time* in Grimsby resembled a lynch mob. The veteran Labour MP Margaret Beckett was shouted down for not having repaid at least some of the £72,537 claimed for items on a house with no mortgage. In vain did she plead that it costs money to run two houses. Even Sir Menzies Campbell, the Liberal Democrats' courtly elder statesman, was given a hard time for his food bill. People never understood why MPs should eat for nothing, at up to £400 a month in taxpayers' money. If only we all could live on rations like that! The programme drew its largest audience ever. So great was the interest that the next week, in Salisbury, it was moved to prime time and did even better in the ratings. Ben Bradshaw (Labour, Exeter) was given a similar grilling. As one of the panellists I had a front-row seat and was relieved to be out of Parliament and no longer in the line of fire.

The most widely quoted text of the day, even in the *Sun* and the *Daily Mail*, was Cromwell's dismissal of the Rump Parliament on 20 April 1653:

'It is high time for me to put an end to your sitting in this place, which you have dishonoured by your contempt of all virtue, and defiled by your practice of every vice; ye are a fractious crew, and enemies to all good government; ye are a pack of mercenary wretches, and would like Esau sell your country for a mess of pottage, and like Judas betray your God for a few pieces of money. Is there a single virtue now remaining amongst you? Is there one vice you do not possess? Ye have no more religion than my horse; gold is your God; which of you have not barter'd your conscience for bribes? Is there a man amongst you that has the least care for the good of the Commonwealth? Ye sordid prostitutes have ye not defil'd this ancient place, and turn'd the Lord's temple into a den of thieves, by your immoral principles and wicked practices? Ye are grown intolerably odious to the whole nation; you were deputed here by the nation to get grievances redress'd, are yourselves become the greatest grievance. Your country therefore calls upon me to cleanse this Augean stable, by putting a final period to your iniquitous proceedings in this House; and which by God's help, and the strength he has given me, I am now come to do; I command ye therefore, upon the peril of your lives, to depart immediately out of this place; go, get you out! Make haste! Ye venal slaves be gone! So! Take away that shining bauble there, and lock up the doors. In the name of God, go!'

The anti-politics mood that swept through the country, Cromwellian in its fervour, became stronger and more coherent as the further misdemeanours of the fractious crew were exposed. The parties were unable to harness this, although they tried to, for they were surfing a tide of public outrage against many of their members and for which they were held to be partly responsible. They could have prevented this but they had not. Party politics was also in the dock. Groups campaigning against named and shamed MPs reached out to each other through the internet. Websites sprang up like ElliotMustGo and BlearsMustGo. A wildfire effect took hold. Elliot Morley (Labour, Glanford and Scunthorpe) did indeed go, or promise to go. Hazel Blears (Labour, Salford) did not. It was no longer enough for the campaigners that the mercenary wretches should apologise. Or wave a cheque in the air and pay back the money. Or agree to stand down at the next election. The people wanted them out *now*, so that they should not enjoy the soft landing and generous resettlement grants that would go with the few months' extra service. Among these groups, the example of Tatton in 1997 came to be widely quoted. I could claim no personal credit for this, since the Tatton campaign was something that I did not originate but bore me along; and party politics was involved in it at the outset, although not in the outcome. But it showed what was possible when the people banded together and cried 'Enough!'

At the start of the scandal, emails were pouring in to the *Daily Telegraph*, the source of the revelations, at the rate of more than one a minute for hour after hour. The paper received 1,500 letters in a single day. The Letters

Editor, Christopher Howse, wrote: 'Never in its 154 year history has the *Telegraph* heard from so many of its readers. Theirs is the voice of a Britain that cares, but is seldom raised in anger.'[2]

My successor as MP for Tatton, George Osborne, bravely faced his constituents in a lively session at the public library in Wilmslow. According to the *Wilmslow Express*, they were unhappy about the £440 he had claimed for a taxi journey to London. He had dutifully paid the money back. 'I have been embarrassed by some of the things I have read in the papers,' he said, 'I have come here today because I wanted to give constituents the first possible opportunity to explain how I thought the system had failed. I apologise as an MP and for abuses of the system.' But it was common practice for MPs to blame the system rather than themselves, and his constituents did not let him off so lightly. One of them, a magistrate, said he had voted Conservative for 40 years, but would not do so again: 'I have just sent someone to prison for four months for theft in a position of trust. Give me some prosecutions against MPs.' Another said: 'What you are giving us is a choice between voting for one bunch of crooks and another.' And a third: 'How scary is it that as Shadow Chancellor you keep making decisions that are wrong?' And this was before they knew he had flipped his homes.[3] George's rise from backbencher to Shadow Chancellor has apparently been effortless; but the more I have been impressed by his political talents the more I have wondered about his common sense.

A friend who had helped me in another campaign called from Essex to tell me of a rebellion against Eleanor Laing, Conservative MP for Epping Forest. Hers was by no means the most egregious abuse of the system, but her constituents were up in arms. She lived 35 miles from London and represented thousands of commuters. She was not however a commuter herself. She had claimed £80,000 of public money towards mortgage payments and service charges on two adjacent flats in London which she named as her second home. Then when she sold them they conveniently became her first home, and she was not liable to capital gains tax on a profit reported to be £1 million. This practice was widespread in the House of Commons but not outside it. No one else in Epping Forest could dance with the taxman like its elected representative. It is of course a privilege to be an MP, but in the opinion of many it should not perhaps be quite so much of a privilege. There were questions of fairness to be answered. Eleanor Laing said she under-stood the people's anger and was raising a bank loan to pay back £25,000 in tax, as her party leader required her to do. I suggested to my friend in Epping that, now her expenses were in the public domain, she could be open to challenge by an Independent. I recommended a campaign on the 'local hero' model of Dr Richard Taylor, representing the Hospital and Health Concern Party in Kidderminster, who had defeated the two main parties and won by a 17,000-vote majority in 2001. If the people were happy with Eleanor (whom I had rather liked) they could vote for her. If not, they would have an electable alternative. It was the best democratic solution. She thanked the voters who had stood by her, but said it had been a horrible experience.

Eric Pickles, Conservative MP for the neighbouring constituency of Brentwood and Ongar, found himself in a similar ... well, pickle over expenses. (I have an interest to declare here: although I am actually rather fond of Eric, who is by no means your run-of-the-mill pin-striped Tory, I challenged him in 2001 and lost by a modest margin.) Like Eleanor Laing he represented commuters but was not himself a commuter. He had a second home near Westminster. Early in the scandal, when it was still in its bath plug phase, he appeared on the BBC's *Question Time* and was heckled robustly when he tried to defend this practice. 'If I can make a contribution to "hang an MP week" ...' he began, and was instantly shouted down. He then talked of the long hours and difficult work. 'Like a job?' asked David Dimbleby. 'Yes, like a job', he said. He later watched a video of his performance, which he compared to a slow-motion car crash. The experience had changed his mind, he said, and put him on the side of the reformers. Unlike many, he understood quite soon the strength of public feeling. As his former opponent in Brentwood and Ongar (I just about won Brentwood but lost Ongar), I am an unlikely member of the Eric Pickles fan club: but he is an astute and accomplished politician who deserves credit, as chairman of the Conservative Party, for taking it in the direction of a new and more open politics. 'Democracy's rather a good thing', he said disarmingly.

He was not alone. The sheer force of the public response to the scandal was changing the minds of established politicians. Defenders of politics-as-usual, who warned darkly of mob rule, would disregard the mood of the people at their electoral peril. If they did not understand it they would suffer from it. It was not violent but it was angry, united and determined. Among the outcomes of the scandal could be an overdue revival of democracy. The voters were taking an unprecedented and unsettling personal interest in their elected representatives. As former President Richard Nixon is reputed to have said: 'Politics would be one hell of a good business if it weren't for the goddamned people!'

These days I seldom visit the Palace of Westminster, since from past experience I tend to regard it as something close to enemy headquarters. But one day during these upheavals I was in the Pugin Room having coffee with a co-conspirator, the pioneering Douglas Carswell, Conservative MP for Harwich and Clacton. As we left, a new Member who was a complete stranger gently reproached me for making too much of a fuss over Members' expenses. 'We're all being tarred with the same brush,' he said, 'and you know, we're not all like that.' A short time later he was revealed to have charged for rent on a second home which, under the rules, he should not have done. Game, set and match.

One of the incidental pleasures of it all was watching the discomfiture of those commentators who proclaimed the merits of the system and the honesty of all but a few MPs. The three musketeers of the political class were John Rentoul of *The Independent on Sunday*, Steve Richards of *The Independent* and David Aaronovitch of *The Times*, who had something else in common: they had all worked at one time or another in the BBC's political office on Millbank (Aaronovitch had actually been in charge of it). And there, in that hotbed of cold feet, they had developed their Pravda-like tendencies. In a contest between the political class and the people, they could hardly defend the politicians any more, so instead they attacked the people. The Iron Cross for a fighting retreat went to the unsurpassable John Rentoul: 'It would be wrong to short-circuit the constitution just because a minority of MPs are thought to have behaved dishonourably in claiming expenses. British government is not a talent show where trivial errors are punished with permanent despatch to the outer darkness with haste. If this is how democracy is supposed to work, I'm off to the Priory.'[4]

It didn't concern him that the supposed minority of MPs included half the Shadow cabinet and three-quarters of the cabinet, that the trivial errors included outright fraud and deception, and that these abuses were not just thought to have happened but actually had happened. The documents were authentic, the facts were not disputed, and the MPs identified had not reached for their lawyers. For the system's apologists, the principal message of the crisis seemed to be not that the voters deserved a better class of politician but that the politicians deserved a better class of voter. In the Priory perhaps he could think this through more clearly.

I don't know what it was about my former employers, the BBC – also the former employers of Messrs Rentoul, Richards and Aaronovitch – but they even broadcast a sympathetic radio programme about the trauma suffered by MPs in a time of scandal, as if these characters were not the authors of their own misfortunes. Maybe it had something to do with the BBC's long habit of even-handedness, and its deeply felt need to strike a judicious balance between truth and falsehood, honesty and dishonesty. Or maybe – and this was more forgivable – it was just the good old-fashioned cussedness of the national broadcaster.

Labour Party supporters started receiving identikit messages from their MPs: 'I thought twice about writing this letter because I know how rightly angry people are.' But the letter was as genuine as a two-pound note. The MPs had not even thought once about writing it, never mind twice, because it was drafted for them in party headquarters. That is another sign of the parties' decline: the traffic is all one way. Instead of listening to people, they deluge them with mass-marketed personalised messages. So maybe politics is a performing art like TV news, of which it was famously said that all you need is sincerity – and that if you can fake that, you've got it made!

The storm had still not abated, but rather increased. The sky grew darker and the sea rose higher. The divide remained unbridged between Them and Us. MPs were shell-shocked, waiting in the no man's land of a discredited House for the next rolling thunder of disclosures.

Many who had been named and shamed cancelled their surgeries and stayed away from their constituencies for a while. It was not a good time to be visiting the local supermarket. One who carried on as usual attended a charity lunch and found himself choosing from a menu that included 'mole pie'. He was not amused. MPs were seldom out of the line of fire. A commentator at the British Open described a golfer's wayward shot as 'crooked as an MP's expenses'. Politicians would rather be abused than ridiculed. There was no one outside their magic circle, and its satraps and surrogates in the press, who believed their lament that they were the victims of a witch hunt.

One of the reasons for this was that, in the early phase, there was hardly an expression of contrition or remorse from any of them. They explained that these were relatively minor matters to which they should have paid more attention. They had made a few regrettable mistakes. They were just too devoted to their constituents to have spent enough time on the paperwork. John Gummer, Conservative MP for Suffolk Coastal, had claimed £23,000 for his constituency home in 2007/8. This had helped pay for sweeping chimneys, repairing the central heating and getting rid of birds' nests and moles. He was fully entitled to the central heating repair, but promised to pay it all back anyway. Half would go to charity and the other half to the Fees Office via the Conservative Party. He told the *East Anglian Daily Times*: 'I believe that it is right for every Member of Parliament, however scrupulously he has kept to the rules and however low his overall claim, to take some part of the corporate blame for a system of allowances that has been shown to be fundamentally flawed and yet which he did not adequately seek to reform.'[5] Mr Gummer, a Commons veteran of 34 years, had never made even such a qualified apology before, or come under so much pressure from his constituents. I come from Suffolk and spend some time there. Former supporters, true blue Tories, were seething with indignation and connecting the expenses scandal with a resonant local issue, the advance of supermarkets into country towns like Saxmundham and Halesworth. Most MPs have constituents with grievances against them, whether on planning issues or personal concerns and even obsessions. A questionable expenses claim could act as a force multiplier for those grievances. Under such a siege and in certain circumstances the safest of seats could become vulnerable.

The Conservative leader David Cameron was not popular with his MPs – 'they hate me', he said – but was surely right when he observed: 'To recognise public anger, we must demonstrate some atonement.'[6] The atonement so far was so soft-spoken, it was hardly audible and not much more than a whispered apology: 'Sorry we got it wrong.' Mr Cameron also did some atoning of his own. He paid back £680 charged for repairs to his constituency home, including the removal of wisteria and ivy from a chimney. Apart from these entanglements his own expenses were relatively straightforward, and easier to defend than those of most of his front-bench colleagues. The gale tore through Westminster, uprooting old oaks, but leaving these saplings untouched.

Chapter 4

Off with their Heads!

Some resigned, some were de-selected and others, if there is any justice at all, will be defeated.

Among the first to jump ship were Sir Nicholas and Ann Winterton, MPs for Macclesfield and Congleton respectively. They had illuminated the back benches – if that is the right word – and been part of the landscape of Tory Cheshire for many years – 37 in his case and 24 in hers. Sir Nicholas had once even held the chairmanship of the Health Select Committee until removed by his own party. He was on the Speaker's panel of senior MPs and owed his knighthood not to his own party but to the late Robin Cook, Labour's former Leader of the House, for services to Parliament. There was no more diligent constituency MP. He sang the praises of Macclesfield as if it were the New Jerusalem. I got on well with him. He was always welcome to come into my Tatton constituency, which was next to his, and make considerable speeches at civic events. Sir Nicholas never knowingly under-spoke. I never felt quite so welcome in his, even when visiting Macclesfield Borough Council; but that was because, like many MPs, he was intensely proud and conscious of his turf.

All political careers in the end depend on trust. And trust in the Wintertons began to dissolve because of a neat, if questionable, financial arrangement that they made with the consent of the Fees Office. In 2008 it was revealed that they had transferred the ownership of their Westminster flat to their children, to whom they paid the going rate – £80,000 over four years – in rent. And the £80,000 was of course from the public purse. This meant that they were using taxpayers' money to reduce their exposure to inheritance tax. When this was worked out by their constituents, who enjoyed no such golden advantages, they became rather less widely admired. Sir Nicholas disappeared for a while, most unusually, from the pages of the *Macclesfield Express*. They were deeply hurt by critical press coverage, national as well as local. Newspapers dubbed them 'Mr and Mrs Expenses'. David Cameron called their actions 'indefensible'. But their constituency associations stood by them, and for the time being they clung on to their seats.

Then suddenly, in the third week of the scandal, they announced their intention to retire. They could not maintain the 'hectic pace' of politics, they said, and would spend more time with their family. The letter of resignation made no mention of the expenses issue; but they may have been helped on their way by some of the claims made by Lady Ann to the Fees Office: £67 for a towel rail, £18 for a toilet brush holder, £165 for chair covers and £94 for an iron and ironing board. The couple also claimed more than £11,000 for food. Ordinary people pay for their food out of their taxed income – but MPs are not ordinary people. They represent us but are not representative of us.

In a well-ordered world there should be an advantage to the taxpayer in electing two MPs for the price of one. But that was not the world of the Honourable Members. The Wintertons were soon to be joined in retirement by another married couple.

Julie Kirkbride was a political journalist who had fallen for politics in general and Andrew Mackay, Conservative MP for Bracknell, in particular. In due course she was herself elected as MP for the safe Tory seat of Bromsgrove. Their undoing was an expenses regime which was ingenious but so unwise that they may wonder for the rest of their days how they ever devised it. It did not pass what Mr Mackay later called 'the test of reasonableness'. He identified their London house as his second home, on which the usual allowance could be claimed. She, quite reasonably, named her Bromsgrove flat as her second home; but she then used taxpayers' money to help fund a £50,000 extension so that her brother could live there too. She conceded that her tax arrangements were complicated, but said they were justified by personal reasons of child care. Both homes were taken care of, up to a certain limit, by the taxpayer.

Andrew Mackay was at the time a senior adviser to David Cameron, the Conservative leader. Cameron removed him from that position, in the best Army tradition of his feet not touching the ground, even before the details of his expenses were published. Mackay's seniority did not save him. He was not at the time a front-bencher, but he was the first high-profile casualty on the Tory side. He tried to defend himself at a public meeting in his constituency, after which he claimed that most of the audience supported him. But that was disputed. There were cries at the meeting of 'Give it back', and one voter said: 'I have no wish to be represented in the next Parliament by a thief.' The public pressure was irresistible. Within days he announced his decision to stand down.

Julie Kirkbride held out for longer. The house that she claimed as second home was more plausibly her real second home. David Cameron said that the two cases should be treated and judged separately. But she too was brought down by the force of the voters' anger. A window in her Bromsgrove office was broken by a missile – the first and very minor use of force in the British revolution. A poll of Conservatives showed that 81 per cent wanted her out. A 'Julie must go' campaign was launched and 3,300 people signed a petition demanding her resignation. The papers were seething with local indignation. It was not a media-driven movement, but came directly and unstoppably from her constituents. She never apologised or admitted wrong-doing, but decided to join her husband in retirement. She was later reported to have had second thoughts about that decision, but she had lost the confidence of many voters and it would be hard for her to see off a challenge from a strong candidate and a well-organised anti-sleaze campaign. The Conservatives were also well aware that, while they were reinventing themselves nationally, a revived Bromsgrove issue could have a negative impact nationally. (This had happened before: they believed that Neil Hamilton had cost them 60 seats in 1997.)

Other MPs announced their departures, in some cases because they expected to lose, in some because of the expenses scandal, and in some for reasons unconnected with it except a general fatigue and a sense that the game was over. These included Christopher Fraser (Conservative, South West Norfolk), Beverley Hughes (Labour, Stretford and Urmston), Patricia Hewitt (Labour, Leicester West), Alan Milburn (Labour, Darlington), Derek Wyatt (Labour, Sittingbourne and Sheppey) and Michael Ancram (Conservative, Devizes). However long they had served, and however well, it must have been sad for them to reflect that the Parliament they left was, in the public view, so much more disreputable than the one they joined. Some resigned for no other reason than that they were totally demoralised.

One who stayed and sought sympathy was Sir Patrick Cormack (Conservative, South Staffordshire). He said: 'The fact is that being a Member of Parliament is an extremely expensive business. One is expected to give liberally to all manner of charities, one is expected to attend all manner of events, one is expected constantly to be putting one's hand into one's pocket.'[1] Such was the mood of the people, however, that the Distressed MPs' Assistance Society would not have been a well supported cause.

It was not just a matter of expenses. It was also a lack of confidence in the Commons itself. Graham Allen MP (Labour, Nottingham North), a former whip turned rebel, said: 'Over the years all of us – certainly me in the past twenty years – have subjected ourselves to an incredible amount of self-delusion in thinking that the House of Commons actually meant something, that its powers were important, that it was somehow, if not an equal partner, at least an elderly uncle whose advice could be taken seriously. ... The House of Commons is at best a supplicant to Government.'[2]

If only the dodgy had gone and the decent remained: but alas it was not that simple. The departure of Andrew MacKinlay, the Labour MP for Thurrock, was a loss to the House which had nothing to do with the expenses scandal. His accounts were reasonable: his only extravagance was a £45 set-top box so that he could watch the BBC's Parliament Channel. Politics was his life. He decided to leave because, like Graham Allen, he despaired of Parliament's ability to hold ministers to account. I considered him a role model, the sort of MP who, but for the party allegiance, I would like to have been: he was independent-minded, he never asked a planted question, he did not care what the whips thought of him, and he successfully resisted their attempts to unseat him from the Foreign Affairs Committee. His interests ranged from Gibraltar to the Tilbury Docks. A number of his colleagues had promised him support on a civil liberties issue and then withdrew it under party pressure. 'They just went tribal,' he said, 'their view of Parliament is totally different to mine.' Other departing MPs were disgraced. The Member for Thurrock was simply disillusioned: 'I have been swimming against the tide and you can only do that for so long before you are exhausted.'[3] If Parliament were full of Andrew MacKinlays it would be rather noisy, because they would all be trying to speak at once, but it would be a much better place than it is.

In some of the most conspicuous cases, MPs were brought down by the interest they claimed on phantom mortgages. Even when the mortgages were real, and the interest on them was paid by the Fees Office, MPs could sell their taxpayer-funded homes for a profit which they then did not return to the Fees Office but of course kept for themselves. Even some cabinet ministers did this while living in grace-and-favour residences at public expense. The system encouraged property speculation by people who should have had nothing at all to do with it, not least because of potential conflicts of interest on issues of taxation. And this was a government which was voted into office in 1997 on a promise to restore public trust in public life. Instead it took leave of conscience and duty and presided over what was, in some cases, a politics of personal advantage. And the penalty for its failure was not in doubt. Just like the Conservatives then, New Labour now would be driven from office by a popular recoil against sliding standards and broken promises. Month by month, the government was shedding ministers and losing authority.

The specifics were extremely damaging. Two Labour backbenchers, Elliot Morley, MP for Glanford and Scunthorpe, and David Chaytor, MP for Bury North, had claimed for mortgage interest on their second homes after the mortgage had apparently been paid off.

Morley was a Right Honourable, a Privy Councillor and former agriculture minister. During 2007 he had been claiming for £800 interest a month on his Scunthorpe home although, according to Land Registry documents, the mortgage had been repaid by March 2006. At the same time he was renting out his London house, which he called his main home, to another Labour MP. He said: 'I have made a mistake, I apologise for that and take full responsibility. My priority was to repay, and if I suffer financially as a result of that, I have only myself to blame.'[4] Why he ever did it was left unexplained. Within days he announced that he would stand down.

So did the MP for Bury North in similar circumstances. David Chaytor admitted that he had claimed almost £13,000 in interest payments for a mortgage that no longer existed. Since 2004 he had claimed for five different properties, flipping his claims between them. He said: 'There has been an unforgivable error in my accounting procedures for which I apologise unreservedly.'[5] The discrepancies came to light only in 2007 after the Fees Office asked MPs to provide mortgage documents to back their expenses claims. Up till then, these claims had been taken on trust. The phantom mortgages were thought to be two cases among many. Back in 1997 to 2001, when I was an MP, no documentary evidence was required for a rent or a mortgage. In the gentleman's club of the House of Commons, all it took was a signature on an expense form.

The case of Ben Chapman, Labour MP for Wirral South, was similar, but hard to decipher and by no means the worst. It was a marginal constituency, which he won in a by-election in February 1997 when New Labour was still trying to assure the voters that it was quite unlike Old Labour. The by-election was important, and one of the most expensive ever, because it was a test run for the forthcoming General Election, and Mr Chapman was chosen because he was as far from a scary socialist as you could possibly imagine. He looked and sounded like a bank manager. He was someone they could trust.

Or was he? In the ten months from December 2002, he claimed about £15,000 in expenses for interest on part of the mortgage for his second home that had already been paid off. He had been given permission to do this by the Fees Office, which appeared to have become complicit in an acrobatic reading of the rules. Mr Chapman, like so many others, was unrepentant: 'I maintain that I have done nothing wrong and have acted in good faith and with absolute transparency throughout. The Commons Fees Office have expressed their apologies and regret that the advice they gave me was incorrect.' Typically, it was not his fault but someone else's. But the publicity had been extremely hurtful and he decided to retire from politics.

The conduct of Hazel Blears was more conspicuous, both because of her seniority – she was Minister of Communities and a former Labour Party chairman – and because of its political effect on a fading and flailing government. The MP for Salford was a long-standing activist and grass-roots campaigner. She and I had something in common: we had both stood against Neil Hamilton in Tatton – she in 1987 and I ten years later. She was vulnerable on the expenses issue, having flipped her second home between three properties and claimed for two television sets in a year. In August 2004 she sold a property in Kennington for £200,000, making a profit of £45,000. It was named as her first home and was therefore not liable to capital gains tax. Gordon Brown called her conduct 'totally unacceptable'. She paid back £13,000 and waved the cheque in front of the cameras, as if that were the end of the matter. (Since it was declared as her first home she was legally entitled to the £13,000, and the Revenue might not have been entitled to collect it.) All that mattered, she explained, was her work for

Salford and what its people thought of her. Her relationship with the Prime Minister was clearly strained, and on 3 June 2009 she resigned from the cabinet though not from her seat. 'I am returning to the grass-roots,' she said, 'in order to help the Labour Party reconnect with the British people.' There was a lot of reconnecting to do. It was the eve of the European election and the party was sinking in the polls like a rock in a pool. Later, Hazel Blears admitted making a mistake in the timing and the manner of her departure. It was unwise as she left to have worn a brooch engraved with the words 'Rocking the Boat'. There were stirrings against her even in her constituency Labour Party. The people were as angry in Salford as everywhere else. A community newspaper, the *Salford Star*, launched a 'Hazel must go' campaign. Within her constituency association she faced a move to de-select her; and survived it by 33 votes to twelve. It was hardly a ringing endorsement from her Labour Party loyalists. The 'Hazel must go' campaign was looking for a suitable local candidate to stand against her. Her re-election was by no means assured. A former safe seat was now marginal.

Then there was the Keith Vaz issue. There quite often is a Keith Vaz issue. It is seasonal, traditional like Beefeaters and Yeomen of the Guard, and one of the recurrent themes of our parliamentary life. In 2001 he was suspended from the House for a month after a complaint against him had been investigated by Elizabeth Filkin (he called it her 'last hurrah'). The Committee on

Standards and Privileges censured him for his refusal, at one point, to answer any more of her questions. He had answered enough, his word was his bond, and therefore her enquiries were superfluous. Mr Vaz, Labour MP for Leicester East, has since been restored to favour. He is a serious and successful politician. He is now chairman of the Home Affairs Select Committee. In July 2007 he was appointed to this powerful post directly by the government rather than through the usual consultative process with the other parties. In 2008, to the government's advantage, he changed his mind to support its policy on the issue of 42 days' detention without charge. The Chief Whip, Geoff Hoon, notoriously sent him a handwritten note thanking him for his help and expressing the hope that it would be suitably rewarded! (The exclamation mark was in the note.)

Arise Sir Keith ... It has not happened yet, but stranger things have. One was his claim for more than £70,000 in allowances over four years for a flat in Westminster when his family home was a house in Stanmore, twelve miles away on the Jubilee Line. Individual items included £480 for 22 cushions, most of them silk, from John Lewis, £1,000 for a dining table and chairs, and £2,614 for leather chairs and a footstool from John Lewis. John Lewis was the store of choice for the Commons authorities and most of those MPs who never knowingly under-claimed. Keith Vaz also flipped his second home twice in a year from Westminster to Leicester and back again. And in June 2009 he paid back £18,949 to the Fees Office, including the cost of those cushions, without giving a reason but so that the public could rest easy. He had done neither more nor less than many others, but was more prominent and influential than most.

The guidance of the Parliamentary Green Book is unambiguous: 'MPs should avoid purchases which could be seen as extravagant or luxurious.'

Yet amid all the unfortunate slips of the pen and inadvertent accounting errors, there was no known instance of an MP making a mistake and claiming too little. It was not always thus. The great Machiavelli was once suspected of embezzlement by the authorities in Florence. When they investigated, they found that they owed him money.

Chapter 5

Black Thursday

Just when you thought things could not get worse, they did. The day that ruined whatever reputation for honour the House of Commons still held was 18 June 2009, about the middle of the second month of the scandal. This was the day when, reluctantly and under pressure, the House of Commons finally published details of its Members' expenses. It was to have been a day of openness, transparency and a brave new world in the MPs' dealings with the wider public. That was what the government and the House said they were committed to. Instead, it was a day of deceit, obscurity and blackness representing the 'redacting' or editing out of embarrassing details which were already in the public domain. The citizens' revolt was by this time in full swing. A quarter of a million people logged on to the House of Commons website on this one day, and could see for themselves the discrepancy between what the MPs had claimed (in some cases, fraudulently and even criminally) and what they had admitted to (not very much of anything, because a proliferation of black rectangles covered it up). We could compare what we knew with what they wished us to know – two very different things. If there was any trust in the process remaining, this was when it seeped into the sand. There was no excuse, but only shock and shame.

At a stroke and on a single day, the House of Commons blackened its reputation with a further blow from which it will take years to recover. Sir Philip Mawer, a former Commissioner for Standards, described it as a classic example of how not to handle a crisis. It was a self-inflicted public relations disaster which made you wonder, what on earth were they thinking of? How did they imagine that those inky pages would look to the voting public? The sheer foot-in-the-mouth and head-banging stupidity of it was breathtaking. Politicians are probably more ruthless and naturally less collegial than the rest of us, since they believe that they have to succeed at each others' expense, but are not necessarily more venal and corrupt. But that was how they appeared. If you ask any group of people to help themselves to money that strictly speaking isn't theirs, many of them will take it. If you ask them to admit to it, they will cover it up. MPs alone had this opportunity. And hundreds of them seized it. Even if they wished to, they were not allowed to publish their expenses in unredacted form.

Only a month earlier, on 17 May 2009, Gordon Brown had declared: 'Transparency to the public is the foundation of properly policing the system.' Yet there was nothing transparent about the publication of thousands of documents all of which were censored and some almost completely blacked out. On the initiative of the old guard, led by Dr Julian Lewis, Conservative MP for New Forest East, the House had voted, on the grounds of security, to keep the addresses of its Members secret. They were public figures with private addresses. That meant that the details of their travel expenses would be blacked out. So would the details of their second homes, and of goods and services delivered there. But for the earlier revelations of the uncensored expenses, the dubious practice of flipping homes would never have come to light. Nor would the phantom mortgages. Nor the duck island, the moat and the mole traps. Entire pages were completely deleted. MPs were encouraged to censor their expenses: and they did it as if their futures depended on it, which of course so many did.

Still some of them didn't get it. After one of my conspiracy meetings I came across Dr Lewis in the central lobby of the House. He looked pale and almost shell-shocked. He thought it unfair that he had been pilloried by the *Telegraph*, which was and remains a viscerally Tory newspaper. I tried to be sympathetic but was probably the wrong man to console him. He is one of a handful of genuine eccentrics in the House. He seeks out unpopular causes and pursues them with a unique blend of courage and cussedness. I do not doubt that he has many fine qualities that endear him to the voters of

New Forest, but seeing himself as others see him is not one of them.

More than anyone else, even fully paid-up members of the old guard like Stuart Bell MP and David Maclean MP, he was the author of the heavy-handed blacking-out of MPs' expenses claims. So great was his passion for secrecy that he even found a way of appearing on the electoral roll in New Forest under an alias. No one knew where he lived; and in due course no one would know where all the other MPs lived either. For in July 2008 the government backed his motion, signed by 256 MPs from all parties, preventing MPs' home addresses from being published under the Freedom of Information Act. The ban included their expenditure on security and the details of goods and services delivered to them. This was the origin of the notorious censorship – *redactio ad absurdum* – that did so much damage to what remained of public trust in public life.

Julian's campaign had nothing to do with his own expenses, which were impeccable, although he did ask about spending £5,595 on wooden flooring with acoustic underlay: 'It could be seen as extravagant', said the Fees Office. He sincerely believed that MPs lived threatened lives and that the idea of revealing their addresses was, as he endearingly put it, barking mad: 'If there is any sense in our having the expensive and complex screening arrangements in the Commons to ensure that nothing horrible, explosive or contaminated is sent in the post *en masse* to Members of Parliament, who are probably being targeted not individually but as a body, it is obvious madness to reveal the 646 home addresses.'[1]

To be fair to Dr Lewis, he raised the issue of the secrecy of MPs' addresses out of what he felt was an understanding of the terrorist's mind and a genuine concern for the safety of his colleagues: 'My concern has been, from beginning to end the insane folly, from a security perspective, of publishing these addresses. This is completely unaffected by the expenses scandals of a greater or lesser nature that have emerged.'[2] He was not a defender of the dodgy dealings of certain of his colleagues. Like many Members, he had no idea of the extent of their wrong-doing. He believed that the notorious flipping of homes could have been caught if just the first three digits of the postcode were published and not the MP's full address. His campaign for secrecy got entangled with an issue which, in his view, had nothing to do with it.

One can admire the man without accepting the argument. Indeed it is possible to see Julian Lewis as a sort of heroic figure in all this. By standing up for the rights of others he drew attention to himself. People wanted to find out more about him. The MP with the most Googled expense claims was not the man with the moat, the man with the duck island or the man with the silk cushions, but the innocent and reclusive Member for New Forest East.

It is important to the public to know where MPs live, and what can be reasonably identified as a first or second home. Without that information they can get away with claiming what they like where they like. So it was with Kitty Ussher, MP for Burnley, who would not have had to resign as a junior Treasury minister if only the redacted version of her expenses had been available. She was clearly not very happy with her constituency home. She asked the Fees Office to pay for £20,000-worth of renovations: 'Most of the ceilings have Artex coverings. Three-dimensional swirls. It could be a matter of taste, but this counts as "dilapidations" in my book! Can the ACA pay for the ceilings to be plastered over and repainted?' The Burnley house with its swirling ceiling was her second home. But in 2007 when she sold it, the property became her principal residence for just one month, enabling her to avoid up to £17,000 in capital gains tax. When this became known she decided to resign not just as a minister but as an MP.

There were long careers cut short by the scandal. Hers was one of the short ones. She had taken the modern route into politics, from researcher and special adviser to others to becoming an MP herself for a safe Labour seat. She was in her first term and one of her party's rising stars. But the swirling ceiling did for her. Her career was over, suddenly and unaccountably. So it happened that some of the perpetrators joined the ranks of the victims. What the old hands and the new-comers had in common – perhaps it was in the DNA of the political class – was what seems to have been an extraordinary recklessness in making their claims, as if rules applied to others but not to themselves. Plus a passion for home improvement, a common sense bypass and a general feeling of entitlement. Either it came from working in a Palace, or the young were being tutored by the not-so-young about how to work the system.

Let it never be said that our MPs were not worth it. As entertainers they should have played the music halls: they were in a class of their own. Even partly censored, the documents included moments of high comedy. George Osborne (Conservative, Tatton) claimed £47 for two DVDs of one of his own speeches – about giving taxpayers value for their money. In the same vein, Ed Miliband (Labour, Doncaster North) spent £35.36 on pictures of himself in a parliamentary debate, and his brother David Miliband (Labour, South Shields) on pictures of himself line-dancing. The otherwise frugal Ann Widdecombe (Conservative, Maidstone and The Weald) spent £9,000 in four years on press cuttings about herself. Ed Balls (Labour, Normanton) claimed £48.50 to sponsor a ball at Ossett Town Football Club. Ben Bradshaw (Labour, Exeter) paid £20 for an engineer to plug a cable into his television. Sir Michael Spicer (Conservative, West Worcestershire) claimed £620 for the installation of a chandelier. David Tredinnick (Conservative, Bosworth) sought reimbursement of £125 for a course on 'intimate relationships'. Richard Spring (Conservative, Suffolk West) spent £39 on copies of the *Racing Post* – which was easier to justify since his constituency includes the Newmarket racecourse.

A special mention in dispatches was earned by Stewart Jackson (Conservative, Peterborough), who claimed £66,000 for his family home, including £304 for work on its swimming pool. He said: 'At all times I have abided by the rules. The pool came with the house and I needed to know how to run it.' Peterborough's MPs, Labour and Conservative, past and present, have shown a rare talent recently for making the news for the wrong reasons. The pool that 'came with the house' raised a few eyebrows. It was almost as if he bought the house and then discovered that it had a swimming pool in the grounds. So of course he would need to know how to run it. And the obliging taxpayers could be expected to help him out.

The Master of the Queen's Music, Sir Peter Maxwell Davies, was so impressed and outraged by the entire scandal that he said he intended to put it to music – 'Expenses: the Opera'. He added: 'The set may have some duck houses and moats in it. I may even invite a few MPs to the opening night. They will of course want free tickets, but be able to claim them on expenses for some fictitious fee.'

What surprises there were! I never met an MP who seemed less of a champagne socialist than Ian McCartney, the former Labour Party chairman, who describes himself on his House of Commons notepaper as the Socialist MP for Makerfield. But there he was claiming for an eighteen-piece dinner set, champagne flutes and wine glasses. He held meetings at his home when he was a minister, he said: 'I had to feed people.' I got to know Ian when I became an MP and he kindly introduced me to some of his friends in the House. He came from a strong Labour background. No one worked harder for his party or his constituents. Like so many others, he was carried along by the trade winds of an expenses regime that should never have lasted for twenty minutes, let alone twenty years. He had also suffered from poor health; and he too decided to leave the House of Commons.

And what to make of the batting averages? What did it say of the state of the parties that the average food claim by a Labour MP was £561, for a Conservative £402, and for a starving Liberal Democrat a mere £210? Why indeed did they charge for their food at all? Was this what they meant when they complained about living on rations? The Tories were unchallenged as the fixtures and fittings party. They knew how to live: good taste does not come cheap. Their average expenditure on soft furnishings was £618, well ahead of the Liberal Democrats on £538 and Labour on an unimpressive £448. The impoverished Lib Dems topped the list on rents and mortgages at £2,818, with the Tories second on £1,938 and Labour third on £1,306. MPs of the minor parties also made some extravagant claims, but generally received less attention. But here at last was real transparency, and the figures ricocheted round the global blogosphere. Some observers were envious.

Disgusted of New Delhi commented: 'We NEED this in India!'[3]

One of the most intriguing questions from the start had been: How many? How many of the 646 MPs had claimed and been paid money from the Fees Office which properly belonged to the taxpayer and not to them? The defenders of the status quo put them at just a handful, the few rotten apples in the barrel. Back in 2002, Speaker Betty Boothroyd observed: 'One has only to have one or two bad apples in a barrel and the public think that everybody is tainted with that same disease.'[4]

We were talking by now of more than one or two. I had at first reckoned in scores, but then in hundreds. For at this stage of the game, when we were past the bath plugs and duck islands and into the black rectangles of the redacted expenses forms, the true scale of the frauds and deceptions was coming to light. By that time, no fewer than 183 MPs had paid back a total of £478,616 to the Fees Office, with no explanation of why it was claimed in the first place or why it was returned. A veil of discretion hung over everything, as if the House was no more than a private club and this was private money. The Commons authorities, addicted to redaction, insisted on keeping many of the details secret. The sums paid back were not just a few pounds and pence. Phil Hope paid back £41,000, Elliot Morley £36,000, Barbara Follett £32,000, and Jonathan Djanogly £25,000.

The parliamentary expenses scandal of 2009, like most political scandals of which Watergate was the primary example, came in two packages. The first was the original wrong-doing. The second was the attempt to cover it up. Each was served up with a powerful set of images. The images of the first were the duck island, the moat and the mole trap. The images of the second were thousands of pages of blanked-out expenses forms which positively cried out 'Guilty as charged'. People did not need to understand the finer points of the expenses system, the Green Book or the Alternative Costs Allowance. The black rectangles splashed across every page, and then the front pages of every newspaper, were themselves a sort of charge sheet. The message they sent about the conduct of MPs was powerful, if over-simplified: 'They are all of them at it, and they don't want you to know!'

The case for MPs hiding from the public goes all the way back to the IRA's bombing campaign on the mainland. Two MPs were killed, Airey Neave in 1979 when a bomb exploded in the House of Commons car park, and Ian Gow in 1990 when a bomb was placed under his car in the driveway of his home in East Sussex. Both men had responsibility for the Conservatives' policy on Northern Ireland at the time. Mr Gow's address was common knowledge and listed in the telephone directory.

A situation might arise when MPs face a similar threat and their protection can then be reviewed. That time has not yet arrived. London is not Kabul or Mogadishu. Special arrangements are made anyway for senior government ministers, many of whom have well-protected grace-and-favour homes, and for some others. The police are aware of MPs' addresses and the need for special measures from time to time. During my own term as an MP, in April 1999, the Cheshire police mobilised their entire armed response unit after I received a death threat which they believed to be credible: and if they believed it was credible, so did I. It was unnerving, but all I had to do was to cancel a single engagement, the opening of a show home in Wilmslow. An attack on Nigel Jones, Liberal Democrat MP for Cheltenham, and the killing of one of his assistants by a constituent armed with a samurai sword, also highlighted the potential dangers faced by all MPs, who are more likely anyway to die in a road accident than at the hands of an assassin.

It is easy to imagine why otherwise well-qualified people might be deterred from going into politics because they would not wish their private lives, past and present, to be exposed to scrutiny and ransacked by the press. It is harder to imagine why they would be put off by the very minimal risk of being attacked by terrorists. Nor would even a reformed House of Commons, quieter and more collegial than the present bear-pit, be a suitable home for such cold and timid souls. I have known some world-class intimidators in my time. Occasionally – as once, for instance, on Knutsford Heath – I beat a tactical retreat. Usually I bashed on regardless. In a democracy like ours, politicians should be afraid of no one but the voters.

The IRA's bombing campaign is over. Anyone who is sufficiently determined can find where an MP lives, even when the address is not listed. A degree of potential harassment goes with the job. We live in an open society where to be a public figure of any kind involves a small but incalculable element of danger. The risks to that society as a whole are, in my view, much greater if MPs hide from the public or use the threat, whether real or perceived, to protect themselves from scrutiny. This applies especially to their parliamentary expenses. It seems cowardly and undemocratic. It suggests that they have something to conceal – as in the case of the redacted expenses records so many of them did. The black rectangles were a self-inflicted wound.

Chapter 6

The Honourable Scapegoat

The last name I had expected to see on the list was that of Dr Ian Gibson, Labour MP for Norwich North. We came into the House at the same time. I always regarded him, and still do, as a man of the utmost integrity. Unlike so many he had a real life before entering Parliament. He was a lecturer at the University of East Anglia, and had once considered a career as a professional footballer. He was not a machine politician who did the whips' bidding, but a free spirit not afraid occasionally to abstain or to vote with the other side. He was sometimes known as the rebel without a pause, but this was unfair: his causes and rebellions were carefully chosen. He was the master of the adjournment debate, the backbenchers' means of holding the government to account on matters of concern to themselves and their constituents. The debate lasts for only half an hour, but the government is obliged to put up a minister to make its case. Dr Gibson knew things that most other MPs did not know: he was the leading authority in the House on a range of scientific and medical issues from GM crops to stem cell research. He was not one of the many MPs who could empty the House, but one of the few for whom others would actually go into it to hear what he had to say.

His offence was not that he lived in his second home, a flat in London, at the taxpayers' expense. He was entitled to that: he could not commute every day from Norwich. It was that he sold the flat to his daughter at half the market price. If he had sold it outright and kept the profit, as had so many of his party's senior flippers – Geoff Hoon, Alastair Darling and (initially) Hazel Blears, to name but three – he would be deemed to have acted within the rules and have been in no trouble at all. As it was, he was summoned before the Labour Party's Star Chamber, its tribunal for dealing with the most serious cases, like those of MPs accused of claiming for non-existent mortgages. He had no place in that company. Yet he was shown the door even ahead of Jim Devine, Labour MP for Livingston, who had charged for repairs to his second home by a company that appeared not to exist. On the Richter scale of the sins of his colleagues, Ian Gibson's error of judgement hardly registered as a tremor.

The Star Chamber de-selected him before any of the others, in a judgement that appeared to have been made in haste so that the party, outflanked and outwitted by the opposition, would be seen to be cleaning out the stable. (In the view of many, it actually *was* the stable, or a substantial part of it.) Ian Gibson said it was not clear to him what rules he had contravened: 'If I knew what

I had done wrong, I could fight back.' He was popular and widely respected in Norwich and Norfolk. He tried at first to appeal to his constituents, who would certainly have supported him, but the party wouldn't let him. So he resigned to force a by-election. The chairman of his constituency association, Martin Booth, who had accompanied him at the hearing like a 'prisoner's friend' at a court martial, resigned from the party. He said: 'It wasn't a Star Chamber – it was a kangaroo court.' Charles Clarke, the other Norwich MP, agreed. He said: 'This incompetent and unjust style has deeply damaged independent politics.'[1] Like many others I wrote Ian Gibson a letter of support. His career had been ended cynically and without due process. He had been made a scapegoat while others much more culpable were free to remain in office, or even resign from it as the spirit moved them, but still to draw their allowances until their time was up. It was difficult to know, as it always had been, what any of these people stood for except re-election. The sheer injustice of it confirmed my long-held view that Labour had a moral vacuum where it should have had a heart.

The editor of the MP's local paper, the *Eastern Daily Press*, with whom he had often crossed swords, or rather pens, confessed to shedding a tear at his departure. 'If it was payback time for his opponents,' wrote Peter Franzen, 'Ian Gibson did not deserve this. This is a fearful state of affairs for the Labour Party.'

Ian Gibson was a popular MP, and not only in his own party: because of his rebellious tendencies he probably had at least as many friends outside it. Most MPs tend to over-estimate their personal popularity, but he had one of the biggest personal votes in the country. If he had chosen to stand as an Independent he would probably have been re-elected with ease. Lord MacGregor, the former Conservative MP for South Norfolk, was one of his many admirers: 'I thought the way in which he was treated was utterly disgraceful and should not have been allowed. I know that the feeling is widely shared in the whole community and in all parties in Norfolk.'[2]

By resigning when he did, Ian Gibson lost his right to a tax-free resettlement grant of more than £30,000, which was half his annual salary. Other MPs – even those facing investigation by the police – made no such gesture in the face of their immediate disgrace and imminent retirement. They hung on shamelessly. They did what they always had done, which was to push every allowance to the limit. Dr Gibson set an example that no one else followed. Racketeering was well rewarded. The out-and-out fraudsters would walk away with a taxpayer-funded farewell. It was as if a convicted con-man, instead of going to jail, spent the rest of his days with a generous pension in a grace-and-favour home. That was not lost on the voters either.

By this time I thought that a total, indiscriminate and Cromwellian purge of MPs was not desirable. The House of Commons needed MPs who knew what they were talking about. It also needed continuity. If all MPs were thrown out who had broken the rules in any way, the House would be as deserted as it looked for most of the time in most of the debates. And the next government, of whichever party, would have difficulty finding enough MPs who were qualified to be ministers.

It is useful here to compare the actions and transactions of different MPs and the penalties that they suffered or escaped. Ian Gibson, Labour MP for Norwich North, had sold his taxpayer-subsidised property and been driven out of politics. George Osborne, Conservative MP for Tatton, had done much the same and sailed serenely on. The difference was that he had not sold it to his daughter. In 2006 Mr Osborne was reported to have made a profit of £748,000 on the sale of his London home. Because it was designated as his main home he paid no capital gains tax on the profit. But for two years he had named it as his second home, subsidised in part by public money, while his main home flipped to Cheshire. It was doubtless not intentional, but the Fees Office had helped both Dr Gibson and Mr Osborne to benefit from a rising property market. One of them was left with his career in ruins. The other continued to prosper.

Neither of the major parties appeared to be applying the same set of rules to all its Members. The Tories' old guard were swiftly cut loose, while their young hopefuls were treated more leniently. In three scandal-scarred months not a single front-bencher was required to step down on either side of the House. That is the way it goes in politics. The big battalions hold their ground while the little platoons are scattered and dispersed. Paul Tyler, a former Liberal Democrat Chief Whip in the Commons, observed in the Lords: 'It is particularly unfortunate than an impression has been given that well-established parliamentarians – who perhaps have a reputation for independence, even unconventional and inconvenient independence – have been those who have been asked to go, while others who are more subservient remain.'[3]

The Labour Party later back-tracked on its Star Chamber, allowing a right of appeal and enlarging the group which decided which MPs should appear before it and which should not. The choices had seemed arbitrary. Why Ian Gibson, for instance, and not Hazel Blears – except that Dr Gibson was a free spirit and she had formerly run the party machine? But by then it was too late. The party had done itself great and avoidable damage. In the after-burn of the expenses scandal, when all that was needed was common sense, it appeared to have made every mistake in the book and then, for good measure, added a few of its own. And a further question arose, since it was the party of government: If it managed its own affairs so incompetently, how could it manage ours?

A number of people in Norwich and Norfolk contacted a friend, a public figure whom I greatly respect, to ask me to stand as an Independent in the by-election following Ian Gibson's resignation. I certainly have the local connections (we Norwich City supporters have had a hard time of it lately). I had even been to school at Taverham in the constituency. And I could probably have counted on the editorial support of the *Eastern Daily Press*, with which I have political and family connections. But I and many others felt very strongly that Dr Gibson himself should have stood as an Independent; and we advised him to do so. He did not, because of the old Socialist Worker in him and a residual loyalty to the party that had treated him so badly. Also, there was no dragon to slay in the by-election, no dodgy incumbent for the people to rise up against. This would become an important consideration in the months ahead. It would not be politics as usual in Norwich North, but it would be politics reshaped by the scandal. The Conservatives had a strong local candidate, as did the Liberal Democrats. The Greens would also offer a principled challenge. Labour was done for. I was tempted, but the circumstances were not right.

The contest in Norwich North was the first by-election since the MPs' expenses scandal broke, and a test of which of the parties would be most damaged by it. Twelve candidates were on the ballot paper, from the major parties, the minor parties and the lunatic fringe, but also including an interesting Independent, Craig Murray, the former British ambassador to Uzbekistan. The people of Norfolk pride themselves on 'doing different', and could not remember ever being offered such a choice. That in itself was good for democracy, but party politics is hard to challenge, even in these days; and Chloe Smith, the 27-year-old Conservative, soon established herself as the runaway favourite. The Shadow cabinet descended on Norwich *en masse*. Labour were not well placed to defend Ian Gibson's 5,459-vote majority, and it was soon clear that it would be something of a political miracle if their candidate Chris Ostrowski, only a year older than Chloe Smith, were to hold on to the seat. It did not help that he went down with swine flu on the eve of the poll ('clearly the gods are angry', wrote his party's vice chair Ann Black later and rather ruefully); but the real reason was the Star Chamber's treatment of Ian Gibson. And Dr Gibson was not on the scene. He could have put in a token appearance, knocked on a few doors, posed for the photographers with his would-be successor, but chose not to. His was the silence of the scapegoat. He owed his party no favours for the brutality with which it had despatched him. As Labour's own *Tribune* observed, the only proficiency that the party displayed throughout the whole sorry affair was the precision with which it shot itself in the foot.

By all the anecdotal evidence, the by-election offered the perfect example of the scandal-driven alienation of the people from the parties. The people wanted to re-elect Ian Gibson, even – perhaps especially – if he had stood as an Independent. The parties offered ABI – anyone but Ian.

The Conservatives won with a majority of 7,348, but on a 45 per cent turnout even they fell 2,000 votes short of their total in 2005. The three main parties between them lost the allegiance of 21,000 voters. The Liberal Democrats fared especially badly: it did not help perhaps that their candidate lived in a house with a moat. UKIP and the Greens did better. Craig Murray, the man from Uzbekistan, could not break the 1,000-vote barrier. ('I was rubbish', he declared disarmingly on his website.) I had warned him that this was the wrong fight for him, and took no pleasure in being proved right. Charles Clarke, the Labour ex-minister who could feel the backwash in his Norwich South constituency, called it a 'coruscating verdict on the way in which Labour has dealt with the issue of MPs' expenses'. If there was any message from this first post-scandal by-election, it was not the victory of one party over another or a general return to politics as usual. It was that the new and powerful anti-politics feeling was unable to find sufficient democratic expression. The people of Norwich North were disenfranchised from voting for the candidate so many of them wanted, the man they called 'Gibbo', their much-loved and wronged MP. When the result was declared, one of them held up a sign that spoke for them all: 'IAN GIBSON – NO VOTES BUT 30,000 HEARTS.'

And this is the democracy we recommend to others, even daring to impose it on distant lands by force of arms?

Chapter 7

Mr Speaker

On the election of Michael Martin as Speaker, I had a cast-iron alibi as someone who was present in the House on the day and who, as the voting lists showed, had nothing whatever to do with it. I had nothing against him personally. He seemed an affable, decent MP from Glasgow, and was a perfectly competent Deputy Speaker, working the tea room and taking the chair while the sainted Madam Speaker, Betty Boothroyd, was elsewhere. It mattered no more to me that he was a former sheet metal worker than that Michael Ancram MP (Conservative, Devizes) was also the Marquess of Lothian (£98, by the way, for repairs to the boiler of his heated swimming pool): it takes all sorts to make a parliament, which is as it should be. What troubled me was that Michael Martin's campaign for the Speakership – or the campaign run for him by his friends – was a distinctly tribal affair. To be effective, the Speaker needs cross-party trust and confidence. Yet against the custom and practice of the House, he was both proposed and seconded by Labour MPs. It

101

was as if the views of the opposition did not matter. His support was almost entirely on the Labour side. As the MPs trooped through the division lobbies, you could palpably sense the hidden hand of the whips. I felt that no good would come of it. And no good did. That was why the alibi was useful.

I rose in the House on 23 October 2000 and said: 'I beg to move, as an amendment to the Question, to leave out "Mr Michael J. Martin" and to insert instead thereof "Mr Richard Shepherd".'

The Commons was crowded, with even Tony Blair in his seat, unusually, for the whole debate, because he had to be. Richard Shepherd was Conservative MP for Aldridge Brownhills near Birmingham, a champion of free speech and civil liberties, a Eurosceptic (he was one of John Major's notorious 'bastards') and a man widely respected on both sides of the House as a principled politician. It was a sign of his appeal that, though he was a Conservative, his sponsors were an Independent, myself, and the respected Labour MP for Cannock Chase, Dr Tony Wright.

I was no great parliamentary orator. But my speech, by chance, was eerily predictive of much that happened later. For even then the House of Commons stood on the edge of disrepute, and most of us knew it: 'The challenges that this House faces have been widely stated. They include an erosion of its authority, reputation and influence by a more assertive judiciary, a more aggressive press and the burgeoning power of the Executive. ... The need is as urgent as ever to restore the dignity and reputation of the House.' And in nominating Mr Shepherd for the Speakership I quoted the Puritan Peter Wentworth in 1575: 'There is nothing so necessary for the preservation of the prince and state as free speech, and without it is a scorn and mockery to call it a Parliament house, for in truth it is none but a very school of flattery and dissimulation.' (Wentworth was sent to the Tower for speaking out too freely against the Crown.)

Tony Wright then spoke: 'I believe that the moment has arrived for a shock to the system. Whatever else my Honourable Friend would be, he would be a shock to the system. … Either Honourable Members believe that we have reached a point where a shock is required, or they believe that business as usual will do. That is the choice. It is no good saying that it will be the job of some future Speaker whom we may elect to put matters right. The job of putting them right rests with all of us in the House now. It is no good talking afterwards of the glories of Parliament and the need for reform, unless we are prepared now to administer a shock to the system that may produce that change.'[1]

Richard Shepherd was not the only candidate to submit himself to the House of Commons that day. Thirteen others included the well-regarded Sir George Young on the Conservative side and the wonderful Gwyneth Dunwoody on the Labour side, who had also asked me to propose her. But the House voted against a shock to the system and for business as usual. *Hansard* recorded: 'The House divided: Ayes 136, Noes 282.' With a few notable exceptions – Vince Cable was one of them – the list of Noes read like a roll call of the government's ultra-loyalists. The Scottish contingent, which included some of the most notorious old bruisers in the House, was solid for Michael Martin, who was one of their own. None of them broke ranks. One of them had even put money on his election. The Labour Party, carrying all before it, had its own man in the chair.

The Speaker holds more absolute power than anyone else in the country. He is responsible to no board of governors or trustees, but only in a general way to the Members of the House. He can silence them by ordering them out or, more frequently, by exercising his right not to call them to speak. MPs know this and seek his favour, bobbing up and down in an attempt to catch his eye. If they fail, they can only be heard at all by intervening on one another – 'Will the Honourable Member give way?' is the cry of the desperate and excluded, or those in search of a quick and easy press release. So Members are unlikely to challenge him; and for more than eight years, no one did.

His office is the hub of the House. It lies at the end of a corridor past the tea room. Members call in there as supplicants, delivering hand-written notes asking for adjournment debates in Westminster Hall, applying to speak in the main debates, seeking an appointment with the Speaker himself or sometimes even complaining about each other. Turf wars between them are common. They also pass through the office on their way to functions in the splendour of his state rooms upstairs, refurbished during his time in office for £1.7 million. The Speaker lives in a palace within a palace. No one declines his invitations. His staff are pivotal people.

The first indication that all was not well was a high rate of turnover among them. The Speaker's secretary was first to go, but others soon followed, including the Serjeant-at-Arms, a former general. No reasons were given, but the word in the lobbies was that the Speaker found them too posh for his liking, and they found him hard to get on with. His use of parliamentary allowances and his employment of members of his own family were also controversial. Having talked to a former member of his staff, I was persuaded to make a formal complaint against him to the then Commissioner for Standards, Sir Philip Mawer. Sir Philip rejected it, because although my informant's credentials were impeccable, he wished to remain anonymous. Had Sir Philip taken the chance, and picked up the phone and made just one call – and he would have known exactly to whom to make it – events could have unfolded differently and a process of reform might have begun before the House was engulfed in the expenses scandal. But it did not happen, and the complaint was never investigated. Mr Martin was also widely perceived, especially by the Conservatives, as not being neutral between government and opposition. He knew where his friends were.

He was also extremely sensitive to criticism. A press campaign against him was launched by Quentin Letts, the waspish sketch-writer of the *Daily Mail*. It was Letts who dubbed Michael Martin 'Gorbals Mick' (which was unfair as well as discourteous, for he actually came from the other side of the Clyde). It passed into the daily shorthand of political journalism. Friends of the Speaker saw the assault as an outrageous act of class warfare, waged by the public schoolboy types of the *Daily Mail*, against a decent man of the people. In face of the attacks Mr Martin hired Carter-Ruck, the libel lawyers, for a substantial fee; and a well-liked spokesman, Mike Granatt, who later resigned after inadvertently misleading a journalist over a story about the Speaker's wife's taxi expenses. Things were getting murkier and murkier inside the Westminster bunker. Newspaper editorials urged his early retirement. *The Observer* thundered: 'The Speaker and Mrs Martin have been plundering the public purse for an almost grotesque array of personal perks and foreign junkets.'[2] But on the credit side, so to speak, in December 2008 Michael Martin won the right to a generous taxpayer-funded index-linked pension until his death.

It was unthinkable that he could survive the expenses scandal. Not only had he presided over the House of Commons at a time of widespread malpractice, but he had led a tenacious rearguard against the disclosures required by the Freedom of Information Act. In this he had the support of the House of Commons Commission and most of the government front bench. But he was an increasingly isolated figure.

One of the newer Tory MPs, Douglas Carswell of Harwich, broke with tradition in criticising the Speaker publicly. This followed a police raid on the House of

Commons office of Damian Green, the Tory spokesman on immigration. The police were investigating the leaks of Home Office files. There was some doubt whether the Speaker, who should have been consulted, had authorised the raid or even known about it. Mr Carswell said: 'The purpose of the Commons Speaker is to preside over an institution that holds government to account – not to give the green light to police raids against legitimate opposition.' He denied any personal malice: 'Kind and affable, according to those who know him, he excels at being Michael Martin. But he is no good at being Mr Speaker.'[3]

On 12 May 2009, when the scandal had just broken, Douglas Carswell put down his first-ever motion as an MP. It expressed lack of confidence in the Speaker. Within days it attracted a dozen cross-party signatures, including that of Richard Shepherd whom I had proposed for the Speakership in what seemed an age ago. The Liberal Democrat leader Nick Clegg then broke with a long tradition of all-party consensus and said that Mr Martin should stand down because he had become an obstacle to the much-needed reform of the House.

It was all but over. The Speaker made a statement to a crowded House apologising for his part in the expenses issue but declaring that all Members were responsible. 'We have let you down very badly indeed', he said. 'We must all accept blame and to the extent that I have contributed to this situation I am profoundly sorry.' He dealt ungraciously with interventions by the Labour MP Kate Hoey, whom he accused of playing to the gallery – he said he had already heard her 'pearls of wisdom on Sky News' – and the Liberal Democrat Norman Baker, a constant thorn in his side.

The next day he bowed to the pressure and stepped down – the first Speaker to be forced out of office since John Trevor, on a charge of corruption, in 1695. Michael Martin's statement lasted just 32 seconds: 'Since I came to this House thirty years ago I have always felt that it is at its best when it is united. In order that unity can be maintained, I have decided that I will relinquish the office of Speaker on Monday 21 June. This means that the election of the new Speaker will take place on Tuesday 22 June. That is all I have to say on this matter.'[4]

The election of a Speaker to succeed Michael Martin was a fractious and confused affair, conducted on the dark side of politics, in keeping with the spirit of the times. The vote was secret, but it was apparently decided for the second time in succession by the Labour majority voting for the candidate of their choice, who this time was not of their own party. But so one-sided was the vote that he might as well have been.

One of the most widely respected potential candidates was Frank Field, Labour MP for Birkenhead, frugal on the expenses issue and a true free spirit who could have been as effective a Speaker as Betty Boothroyd. But he did not stand a chance of being elected. And in the end he did not stand at all. He had probably alienated too many of his colleagues with an unsparing attack on the Prime Minister at a meeting of the Parliamentary Labour Party after the government's hammering in the local and European elections. He described Gordon Brown's premiership as inept and the party's standing as pitiful, which was not the way to win over the Labour rank and file. Frank Field's outspokenness was unusual among professional politicians: he said what he thought, regardless of the consequences, especially to himself. His name did not go forward.

That left ten candidates in the contest, one of whom, Margaret Beckett of the hanging baskets, was said to be the favourite of the government whips. No matter that the whips were supposed to stay out of it: that was not in their nature. Three others were Tory veterans who had tried before and lost to Michael Martin. These three were Richard Shepherd (my personal nominee in 2000), Sir Patrick Cormack and Sir George Young, the bicycling baronet who had come second in 2000 and was about to do so again.

The odd one out – or some might say the oddest in any company – was John Bercow, the Conservative MP for Buckingham. He was only 46 years old, the son of a taxi driver from Finchley, and no grandee but an accomplished politician and the ultimate representative of the political class. He had studied government at Essex University and become national chairman of the ultra-right-wing Federation of Conservative Students, which was closed down by the then party chairman Norman Tebbit, himself no moderate, because it was too extreme. He single-mindedly pursued his ambition of becoming an MP, even hiring a helicopter to travel from one selection meeting to another. Soon enough he found a job as a lobbyist and then political adviser to cabinet ministers in John Major's government. In 1997 he survived the Labour landslide and was first elected. I came into the House at the same time and watched his performances with real astonishment. He possessed skills that were useful in the Commons but nowhere else. He knew more about parliamentary procedure, points of order and ten-minute-rule Bills when he first took his seat than I did when I left mine. He could do it all from memory without a note in his hand. He must have been studying this stuff for years. This knowledge would be useful when he faced his first test as Speaker, which would probably be a procedural challenge by Dennis Skinner. One of a new Speaker's traditional rites of passage is to require the Member for Bolsover to leave the House.

He also shifted, or trimmed, his politics – it was hard to know which. He travelled within his party from the hard right to the soft left, to an extent that most of the Tories wished him to leave and cross the floor. They loathed him. He was thought some years before the event, and as Michael Martin's authority declined, to already have had his eye on the succession. He was manoeuvring for Labour votes and his plan succeeded. Politics is a ruthless business, and maybe it was just his success that the Tories did not forgive. On the third ballot he beat his remaining challenger, Sir George Young, by 51 votes. Most Labour MPs responded tribally to the removal of Michael Martin by installing the candidate who, although a Tory himself, would most upset his party's own MPs. Mr Martin's old nemesis, Quentin

Letts of the *Mail*, who could never be accused of even-handedness, observed: 'They went and did the impossible yesterday. They voted for someone who could be even worse than Gorbals Mick.'[5]

Or he could be just what the House of Commons needs, the 'clean break' figure that he promised to be. It was just that the manner of his victory was partisan. According to a Conservative MP, Nadine Dorries, he secured the votes of only three of her colleagues. And he took office when the reputation of the Commons had never been lower. The people were looking to their MPs for a new beginning, but in a matter as important as the election of their Speaker and the reputation of the House, they were still playing party games and scoring points off each other. 'Do we get it?' asked Parmjit Dhanda MP, one of the defeated candidates. 'Do we understand the level of public anger? I'm not sure that we do.'[6]

In his acceptance speech John Bercow said: 'We have faced the most testing time which has left many Members feeling sore and vulnerable but with large sections of the public feeling angry and disappointed. I continue to believe that the vast majority of Members of the House are upright, decent, honourable people who have come into politics not to feather their nests but because they have heeded the call of public service.'[7]

The vast majority theory was popular among those who judged that the storm would blow over and they could then carry on as they had been, with a little tinkering and some minor reform to the system. The Prime

Minister Gordon Brown and the Justice Secretary Jack Straw were among those who believed, against all the evidence, in the vast majority theory. But the vast majority theory was at odds with the public perception of malpractice by more than a minority of MPs. To take the immediate example: the vast majority of the candidates for the Speakership, eight out of ten, had themselves been diminished in some way by the scandal. Mr Bercow himself was one of these. He had benefited financially from the flipping of homes. Both his constituency home and his London home had been designated as main residences when he sold them, thus removing the burden of capital gains tax. He 'voluntarily' agreed to pay back £6,500 to the Revenue.

The resolution of this would certainly take more than fine words. The speeches made one case but the expenses forms made another. Among a large section of MPs, perhaps nearer to a half than a third of the total, a culture of petty larceny had prevailed which was much like that of HMP Slade in the BBC sitcom *Porridge*. Ronnie Barker's Fletcher would have felt quite at home in the Palace of Westminster. It was even suggested that the best response to the problem of MPs' accommodation was to hire a prison ship, moor it next to the House of Commons terrace, and require MPs to use it as their living quarters, one cell at a time. Then they would be close to their work and could walk the plank every day before each vote.

It did not increase public confidence that one of the first acts of the House of Commons under Speaker

Bercow was to reissue and amend the Green Book which set out the general principles of what expenses should and should not be claimed by the Honourable Members. An interesting addition was inserted, never debated but decided in secret, under the heading of 'subsistence': 'A flat-rate sum of £25 may be claimed for any night which a Member spends away from his or her main home on parliamentary business. No other payment in respect of subsistence may be claimed.' After all that had happened – the shame, the disgrace, the licence to loot and pillage the public purse – here was another nice little earner, of up to several hundred pounds a month, handed out to MPs on a basis of trust and with no receipts required to back it up. Under the new rules some MPs were actually charging more for food than under the old ones. The sheer impenitence of it was extraordinary. The decision was made under the old regime but announced under the new one. The House of Commons, even under its 'clean break' Speaker, had still not lost its capacity to astonish.

There was still more discomfort in store for the new Speaker. Figures obtained under the Freedom of Information Act showed that over a four-year period 60 MPs had received a total of nearly £300,000 from the Fees Office, mostly in payments of £250 a month, under the heading of 'petty cash'. No receipts were required. On top of all the other allowances, it was a useful little extra tax-free cash flow. If I had only known about it, it could have earned me an extra £12,000 during my time as an MP. Most of the beneficiaries were Labour MPs, but one of them was the Conservative John Bercow. They were supposed to use it for casual expenses and hospitality to their Commons visitors – tea, coffee, soft drinks and the like. Some of them – not the abstemious Mr Bercow – certainly spent it in the Strangers' Bar and other watering holes where stronger brews were on offer than tea and coffee. (There was a famous occasion, after one of Peter Mandelson's resignations, when the Strangers' Bar actually ran out of champagne.) Speaker Bercow said: 'Although the arrangement was simple and convenient, I recognise that the climate of opinion has changed and, as Speaker, hold the view that claims without receipts should no longer occur.'[8]

The final act in this soap opera of regime change was the conferring of a peerage on Michael Martin. This too was controversial. In normal times an outgoing Speaker is automatically elevated to the Lords. But in these times? The House of Lords Appointments Commission thought not. All nominations to the Upper House pass through it, which was how the cash-for-peerages issue came into the open in 2007. In a discreet and carefully worded submission to Number Ten the Commission, chaired by Lord Jay, the former Permanent Secretary at the Foreign Office, warned that Mr Martin's elevation to the Lords might damage its reputation. But the Commission did not have the power of veto. Its objections were overruled by the Prime Minister, who was reported to have assured the outgoing Speaker that, if he stepped down, he would follow his predecessors into the Upper House. So the Commons passed a motion urging the Queen to honour Mr Martin 'for his eminent services during the important period in which he presided with such distinguished ability and dignity in the Chair of this House'. The Queen responded with a message to Parliament that she wished to confer on him 'some signal mark of her royal favour'. And so the deal was done.

The Commission clearly took a different view of Speaker Martin's record in office. But it might have seemed vindictive to break with tradition. Besides, he was not so much being honoured for his service to the Commons as rewarded for bringing it to a voluntary end, and so removing himself as a road block to reform. His removal would prove rather easier than the reform.

Chapter 8

The Independent Deterrent

It was a time of popular insurrection against the party politics that had brought about this scandalous state of affairs – much more serious than the sleaze of the Tory years because the stain was more widespread and touched senior politicians of both main parties, with the smaller ones not exempt. The people were not only angered, but *embarrassed*, by the misconduct of so many of their MPs. At a time when so many professional politicians had fallen into disgrace, it was inevitable that Independents and amateurs would have some part to play.

There was already a larger group of non-party MPs in the Commons than at any time since the abolition of the old University seats in 1951. Dr Richard Taylor (Wyre Forest) and Dai Davies (Blaenau Gwent) were both elected as Independents; and in the course of the Parliament they were joined by two Tory MPs and two Labour MPs, including Clare Short, who had fallen out with their parties. They took no whip and were not a party, since a party of Independents is a contradiction in terms, but they did operate as an informal bloc. They consulted with each other; they had a high media profile; and they were listened to, inside and outside the House, rather more than most backbenchers. Richard Taylor, serving his second term, was a respected member of the Health Select Committee. The prevailing public mood of 'a plague on all your parties' was favourable to them. They did not share in the general disrepute. So there was something already in place to build on, if the right candidates could be found for the right constituencies.

In a ComRes poll commissioned by the think-tank Ekklesia, 78 per cent said that Independents should stand where MPs had behaved unethically, and 63 per cent believed that more Independents would strengthen our democracy.[1] And in a *Guardian* poll, 74 per cent said they would consider voting for an Independent.[2]

The first to jump into the fray was Esther Rantzen, who at 69 had been a TV celebrity for as long as many of Parliament's backwoodsmen had been MPs. Typically, she took herself off to Luton South and announced her intention to challenge the sitting Labour MP, Margaret Moran, who had claimed £22,500 of the Alternative Costs Allowance to deal with dry rot in a house in Southampton 100 miles from her constituency. It turned out that Esther, too, owned a house with dry rot, but she had not expected the taxpayer to foot the bill for fixing it. So off she charged to Luton, to take on an

MP who in my view was as strong a candidate as any for de-selection; and who shortly afterwards, without a word of apology, announced her decision to stand down, on the grounds of ill health brought on by the stress of it all. If Esther needed a windmill to tilt at, there were plenty out there, but not in Luton. 'It isn't just about her,' she said, 'it's about the whole lot of them.' I can claim no mastery of politics myself – but, compared to Esther, I am Machiavelli. And this is what Machiavelli, the most influential special adviser ever, said about princes – or in our case, candidates – putting themselves about and being seen by the people: 'He [the prince] should entertain people with shows and festivals. Since every city is divided into guilds and districts, he should respect those groups and go to their meetings from time to time, showing what a humane and generous person he is, though without ever forgetting the authority of his position.'[3] Niccolò Machiavelli's cynicism seems to me to connect directly with our own dishevelled politics. The purpose of power is to stay in power. That is all it is. There is no larger purpose. Machiavelli also wrote: 'If a ruler wants to survive, he must learn to stop being good.' There was no need to tell that to our political class: they had apparently already learned it.

The prospective candidate for Luton South met me a few days later. 'Esther,' I said, 'I think you are going to need a Plan B.' She promised to wrap a cold towel round her head and went away to think about it.

And then she plunged on in anyway. Esther typically took no one's advice but her own. She did not entertain people with shows and festivals, but she did sport a straw boater – a nod in the direction of the town's hat-making industry – and hold a press conference to announce that she would stand as an Independent for Luton South at the next election. She would have been the first to admit that she had little idea of what she was getting into. *Strictly Come Dancing* or *I'm A Celebrity Get Me Out Of Here* were easier than this. Her strength was that she needed no introduction – among politicians she had as much first-name recognition as Boris and Ken. Her weakness was the lack of a tainted incumbent to take out. The Conservative candidate, Nigel Huddlestone, made the obvious point: 'If you're going to stand as an anti-sleaze candidate, surely it would make most sense to stand against an actual wrong-doer.' It was not as if there was any shortage of them. But she had as much right to stand in Luton as anyone else. And she could certainly woo the cameras with the best of them: 'For me it's a bit like going to the moon,' she told *The Guardian*, 'a small step for a woman, a big step for Independents.'[4] The bookies quoted her at a generous 4/1.

Terry Waite's approach was rather more cautious and measured. Former hostages think back and plan ahead. We had talked it over in May 2009 at Wymondham in Norfolk, after the annual memorial service for the former Far East prisoners of war. Like me he had recently turned 70 and was a bit on the elderly side to be one of the piston rods of revolution. But Terry is a serious and principled man. He was as troubled as we all were by the misconduct of literally hundreds of MPs; and not sure what to do about it. But doing nothing was not an attractive option. So he half-mounted his charger and half-threw his hat into the ring with an influential column in *The Times*: 'Parliament is important but not the moribund parliament we have suffered for far too long. The transformation from duck house to dog-house was rapid and took everyone by surprise. Now is the time for the people of this country to rally round those men and women willing to serve their country as Independent Members of Parliament. They won't have all the answers but may well bring some fresh air into a political hothouse that has been suffocating us for too long.'[5]

In politics as in war, time spent in reconnaissance is seldom wasted. An Independent candidature against a vulnerable incumbent is best delayed for as long as possible, lest the regular forces, the party machines, should isolate the challenge and blast away at it. It is thus a political form of guerrilla warfare. I think that Terry knew that, as did other potential candidates who were in contact with him. There was no formal organisation, but there was an informal network of people advising each other and weighing their chances against some of the most vulnerable incumbents.

Terry Waite's obvious target if he chose to go ahead was David Ruffley, the Conservative MP for Bury St

Edmunds, where he lived. Mr Ruffley had made claims for furniture which included a sofa for £1,674 and a bedstead for £3,350. Not all of these were allowed. He admitted that the Fees Office ruling was 'open to question' and canvassed his constituents for their views. The constituents had quite strong views, not all of them in sympathy with their MP. But he also had some support. Most MPs do. It is one of the advantages of incumbency.

Terry Waite had been approached to stand for Parliament before. He came from the village of Styal in the Tatton constituency, and he would have been well placed to take on Neil Hamilton in 1997. It was said locally that he had turned it down on the grounds that he had already served one four-year term as a hostage and did not want to serve another. So the people of Tatton had to turn to someone else.

At this point the possibility of a number of outsiders threatening the status quo really started to alarm the political class and its cheerleaders in the press. Esther and Terry had as much right to stand for Parliament as anyone else, whether or not they were well known. Esther in particular was a magnet for incoming fire. Bloggers railed against her as bloggers tend to, because so often they seem to be ill-intentioned people whose fingers work faster than their brains. Dominic Lawson's headline in *The Independent* set the tone for the newspaper columns: 'The Good Lord preserve us from government by the popular will.'[6] But isn't that just what democracy is about? No less forthright was Catherine Bennett in *The Observer*: 'Government by celebrities? Not if it means Esther is in charge.'[7] A Parliament of celebrities, we were told, would lead to chaos and anarchy. So would a parliament of local heroes in the mould of Dr Richard Taylor, the Independent MP and physician of Wyre Forest. But we were not Jacobins or anarchists. We were not dumb ciphers either. We were people who cared about politics. We would not troop through the lobbies on the orders of a whip – indeed, we would not have one. We had no ambition for red boxes, ministerial limousines or the other trappings of office. All that we were proposing was a House of Commons with a handful of genuine Independents in it, to set an example and help hold the rest to certain standards of honesty. They would act as purgatives of the sickly body politic. They had never been more necessary. They would be single-issue MPs in the sense that they were drawn into politics to help clean it up, but reform of the system would not be their only interest. You can be a single-issue candidate; but, if elected, you cannot be a single-issue MP.

And the champions of party politics still had to explain why, if political parties were so essential to the functioning of good government, the great mass of Tory and Labour MPs had been pressured into defying the wishes of their constituents in March 2003, and voting for an illegal war with such disastrous consequences. The people had marched, and the people had not been heeded. It was not the mainstream politicians but the rebels, smaller parties and Independents who had opposed the war in Iraq. The great apparatus of the parties in Parliament turned out to be not such a public good after all. MPs without a party could consider each issue on its merits and cast their votes accordingly. It was the force of this argument that sent shivers down party spines, where they existed.

As Churchill observed in his great 'locust years' speech of 12 November 1936, it is not a time for panic or despair, but we are entering a period of consequences. Following the expenses scandal, we too are entering a period of consequences. In our case they are a lack of confidence in our MPs and the enfeeblement of our democratic institutions.

The great Independent, A.P. Herbert, who left the House of Commons in 1951, told the story in his memoir *Independent Member* of a Tory old-timer observing the flood of new MPs entering the House for the first time after the Labour landslide in 1945. He stood in the central lobby and was thoroughly alarmed. 'Good God,' he said, 'they look like damned constituents!' For the first time since then, the machine politicians were worried by the prospect of another wave of constituents challenging the old order and becoming MPs themselves. People power – government by popular will – could so easily get out of control. It was unlikely to happen on a similar scale, but something was stirring out there which made them nervous. The political class had reason to man the ramparts with its placemen.

But simply being Independent is not enough. In March 2009 a movement of Independents was launched by an unlikely insurgent, Sir Paul Judge, a former director general of the Conservative Party. He had fallen out with the party and was concerned, like many of us, about the alienation of the political class from the people, and vice versa. He called his movement the Jury Team. The idea was that in each constituency, or region for the European elections, people would vote in an open primary for the Jury Team's candidate; so the candidate would not be imposed, but democratically chosen. The voting would be done by mobile phone, bringing to politics the inter-activity of the TV reality shows. Sir Paul proposed a wide range of constitutional reforms, including single-issue referendums by popular demand. He personally contributed £50,000, and hired some dynamic young people as assistants, to try to make it happen.

It seemed an interesting initiative in providing some support for Independents. Richard Taylor MP, Tony Egginton the Mayor of Mansfield, and I all spoke to encourage it at the launch. We knew from experience how hard it is to stand as Independents, and to compete with the established political parties, except in special circumstances. To succeed, three conditions have to be met. The first is a well known candidate (Dr Taylor is a good example: he ministered to thousands of his constituents as a physician and these were the ones who – as he puts it – survived to vote for him). The second is a good cause. The third is an unpopular and vulnerable incumbent.

There was no lack of vulnerable incumbents in the European elections, and the cause of ejecting them was a good one. But the Jury Team was late in the field and not sufficiently recognised by the voters. It made little impact. One of the lessons of the Jury Team experiment was that an Independent uprising, if there was to be one, could not be structured or organised like the campaign of a regular political party. It was a different animal entirely. The only rule was that there were no rules. It had to be local, spontaneous and serendipitous. If the right circumstances came together – an electable challenger against a disgraced incumbent – anything could happen; and if they didn't, nothing. There was no middle way.

An interesting example was that of Craig Murray, campaigning as an Independent in the Norwich North by-election. He was the former British ambassador to Uzbekistan, who fell out with the Foreign Office over its alleged lack of concern about human rights violations by the Uzbek government. So he resigned and stood against Jack Straw in Blackburn in the 2005 General Election. He ran a spirited campaign from the top of an old fire engine and polled just over 2,000 votes. In his opening rally he gave one of the best political speeches I have ever heard. He made an impact in a one-party town. Yet now, despite having spent £12,000 of his own money on newspaper advertisements, and a DVD sent to every home, he was struggling to make an impact in Norwich. The circumstances were not right. There was no dragon to slay in the housing estates and neat suburban communities of Taverham and Drayton: he lacked a flawed incumbent to defeat. He was third favourite with the bookies; but when Michael Crick of the BBC's *Newsnight* ran a by-election report, Craig Murray did not get a mention even as one of the minor candidates. He called me up in a state of great vexation, since I had campaigned for him in Blackburn: what did he have to do to be taken seriously? I doubted whether human rights in Samarkand would be among the big issues of the Norwich North by-election. But I remonstrated gently with Michael Crick, whom I know quite well. He is a perfectly normal human being until the camera is switched on, at which point he goes into a snarling impersonation of Jeremy Paxman without the sublime *hauteur* of the original. He answered that at that point none of the candidates had actually yet been nominated, and it was hard to know with Independents which of the hopefuls would actually go through with it. But he added: 'The problem of giving fair broadcast coverage to Independents and minor parties has long troubled me.'

The political climate favoured none-of-the-above candidates, but the media mindset did not. It was still all too possible for the voices of credible and serious Independents to be drowned out by the raucous clamour of mainstream politics, and by the party political broadcasts. The parties had an automatic right to a hearing – including UKIP, the Greens and even the BNP, all of which had seats in the European Parliament. The Independents did not. It was all at the whim of the likes of Michael Crick. The broadcasting code, like the electoral system, was not designed for multi-party and non-party politics. In this case an attempt to restrict the coverage of the minor parties – and especially the BNP – had the effect of silencing the Independents altogether. Whatever it was, it was not democratic, but part of a trend to ignore the many voices out there and focus on the few. After I sought election to the European Parliament in 2004 as an Independent for the Eastern Region, a lady wrote to me rather regretfully from some-where in Hertfordshire saying that she did not know I was standing until she saw my name on the ballot paper – and then, supposing that I was an impostor, she voted for someone else!

A group of community activists in Manchester asked me for advice about standing as Independents. They were concerned about gun and knife crime on housing estates sunk in apathy and despair. The city was still largely a one-party state, and they felt deserted by some of their Labour MPs. One was a notorious claimant of luxury items. Another was a junior minister who had flipped his homes and claimed £9,600 in petty cash. A third was Hazel Blears. I told them of the perils and pitfalls of an Independent campaign, and of the fierce opposition they would encounter, but also of the unprec-edented opportunities that were opening up. For days and even weeks of a campaign you can appear to be getting nowhere until just before polling day, when it can suddenly catch fire and become unstoppable. There is no magic formula and no way of knowing if it will work except by trying it. Sometimes it does and sometimes it doesn't. They would receive no automatic votes, but have to earn every one of them. They had nothing to lose but their sense of helplessness. At least they seemed willing to make things happen which, without them, would not have happened. That is the romance of an against-all-odds campaign: it just might work. And indifference, as the great Elie Wiesel has reminded us, is both a sin and a punishment.

Chapter 9

A Personal Decision

The scandals of the Duck Island Parliament left me in a difficult position. I was as appalled as everyone else, and could hardly sit this one out as none of my business. It was everyone's business. I had parliamentary form as an Independent. And because I had once unseated an MP, Neil Hamilton, who was under a bit of a cloud, there were many people urging me to do it again. But against whom? And in which constituency? I was so spoilt for choice that I would not have known where to start. I couldn't walk down the street, go shopping or even pass through airport security without being stopped by strangers asking for an encore. 'Stand again', they said. As the expenses scandal unfolded, I was getting off the 102 bus near my home in north London when a passing motorist wound down his window and called out: 'You shouldn't be on a bus, you should be in Parliament!'

I received a number of invitations, mostly from Independents and other free spirits, urging me to stand in their constituencies, usually against middle-level miscreants, both Labour and Conservative, who had not been shamed into standing down and, if they did not face a serious challenge, stood a depressingly good chance of re-election. The electoral landscape was littered with them. There was no lack of good causes or tainted incumbents. In the old days it was possible to stand for more than one constituency at a time – William Cobbett did it – but those times are long gone. It was of course flattering to be asked, and encouraging that people were taking a serious interest in the conduct of their MPs. They took it as a personal insult to be represented by crooks.

Here is a sample from my pile of letters. 'I was taught right from wrong, and I have lived my life accordingly. Now like millions of other ordinary people, we feel that we have been cheated. *I wonder, sir, have you come back to finish the job you started?*' You had only to look at where we were in the summer of 2009, compared to where we had been in the spring of 1997, to conclude that I had not got very far with the job I started. So was there any point in trying again?

There were a number of reasons to reject the idea out of hand. One was that I would be 71 by the time of the next election, perhaps not as energetic and zealous as when I was 59 and a new MP – and who would want to vote for an old man (except of course for Richard Taylor MP, the legend of Kidderminster, who is even older than I am)? Another was that while I had enjoyed the constituency work first time around, I had found the House itself a bit of a nightmare. I had not felt so stressed in any war zone. I used to count down my 'days to do' like a soldier looking forward to demob. I was initially over-awed by the majesty of the Palace of Westminster, but less impressed by the quality of so many of the Members elected to it. I wondered how they got there. Some were incoherent. Others were drunk. I knew a man in Annie's Bar who drank himself to death; not that the whips cared, so long as he could stagger upstairs to vote. Many were merely mediocre. As the late and great Gwyneth Dunwoody put it in her parliamentary swan-song: 'I have been in the House long enough to see the coming and going of many inadequate personalities. I have seen those on both sides of the House who have been promoted for various reasons. I have seen the crawlers. I have seen those who have used sex – there are so many it would take too long to name them …'[1]

If I was impressed by Parliament when I entered it, that may have been partly because I had hardly set foot there before and knew so little about it. The sense of privilege did not survive the contact with reality. Since June 2001, when I left the House of Commons, hardly a day passed when I did not count my blessings for being out of it. The exception was 18 March 2003, when I wished that I had been present on behalf of the people of Tatton, or Brentwood and Ongar, or anywhere else which would have had me, to vote against the disaster of the war in Iraq. I could hardly believe what the MPs were doing. It was a time of despair.

I had hoped to find the best of British and been disappointed not to. My four years in the House were in some respects the most shocking of my life – so shocking, that when the scandals were revealed I was only half surprised. I had known that things were bad, but not this bad. And to the end of my days I shall never understand why anyone should expect the taxpayer to foot the bill, not only for a fictional mortgage and fancy furniture, but for pork pies and scotch eggs as well.

Then there is the weather of the House of Commons – by which I mean the brooding hostilities of the adversarial system. Behind the ritual courtesies of Honourable Members, Right Honourable Members, Honourable and Learned Members, Honourable and Gallant Members and all the rest of the stately mumbo jumbo, there lies the reality that politics is a profession that rewards aggressive behaviour. It all too often attracts piratical and ill-intentioned people who succeed in unarmed combat at each other's expense, not only between parties but within them. When Neil Hamilton described me as 'a nice enough man but totally unsuited to politics' I hope that he was right; but he certainly didn't mean it as a compliment. I know many decent and admirable MPs. But I see them as the exception and not as the rule. And I believe that the potential malevolence of the place has increased with the rise of the political class. If these professional MPs are defeated or de-selected they have no real-world job to go back to. Having been an MP is not much of a qualification for earning a living elsewhere. So they will do whatever it takes to hang on to the only job they know. The stab in the back is second nature to them.

Nor was the House of Lords, traditionally a retirement home for ex-MPs, available to those forced out of the Commons in 2009, with the notable exception of the Speaker, Michael Martin. The House of Lords had problems of its own, with two of its peers suspended for unethical conduct, and other scandals bubbling beneath the surface. Its Appointments Commission let it be known that the swindlers, flippers and double-dippers from the other House would not be welcome within its stately precincts.

One of the differences between the Lords and the Commons is that MPs tend to waste time by ritually insulting each other and peers by ritually complimenting each other. The brickbats and bouquets are inherited baggage and usually have nothing to do with the business in hand. There are many good reasons for seeking to become an MP, but the quality of parliamentary debate is not one of them.

It has been said that politicians campaign in poetry but govern in prose. In my personal experience that is not true. They campaign in prose but govern in gobbledygook.

Although it is probably more negative than it used to be, there is nothing new in the perception of politics as having something of the night about it. Rudyard Kipling, whose cousin Stanley Baldwin was Prime Minister, used to watch the House of Commons from its gallery and knew more about politics than most: he called it 'a dog's life without a dog's decencies'. And as for standing for Parliament, he had a horror of it which he expressed in some violent lines which he nearly threw away, but were rescued and published by the *Scots Observer* in 1890:

> *My soul! I'd sooner lie in jail for murder plain and*
> *straight,*
> *Pure crime I'd done with my own hand, for money, lust,*
> *or hate,*
> *Than take a seat in Parliament by fellow-felons cheered,*
> *When one of those 'not provens' prove me cleared as you*
> *are cleared.*[2]

Another patriot and poet with his finger on the pulse, G.K. Chesterton, wrote in similar vein in 1912, at the time of another great scandal, the Marconi affair, when ministers were accused of profiting from insider share trading:

> *In the city set upon slime and loam*
> *They cry in their parliament 'Who goes home?'*
> *And there comes no answer in arch or dome,*
> *For none in the city of graves goes home.*
> *Yet these shall perish and understand*
> *For God has pity on this great land.*

Many years later, from an Independent perspective and after one Prime Minister's Question Time too many, I was provoked to write a requiem for party politics:

> *Indifferent to the people's warning,*
> *The parties headed for a fall,*

Tory, Labour and Lib Dem.
At the going down of the sun and in the morning
We will of course remember them,
But miss them not at all.

Despite the avalanche of scandal, party politics is with us to stay. It appears to be necessary for stable government. But though careers depend on it, it does not have to be as ill-natured as it is. An unblemished Parliament is probably not possible. We are flawed and fallible and it is bound to reflect our shortcomings. But a moderately honest and competent Parliament is surely within our reach. To try to gate-crash it is a daunting task for anyone outside the system.

Politics is a bit like war without the comradeship. The metaphor of a campaign comes from the military. In politics as in war, as Gordon Brown was finding out, it is not enough to react to events; you have to take the initiative and shape the battle space, or your enemies will outflank you and your friends desert you. And if you are an outsider, even to set foot there is to risk your reputation and peace of mind, if not your life and limb. Put your head above the parapet and you will certainly be shot at. If you are perceived to have a chance of winning you will be shot at even more. Falsehoods will be invented and repeated. In my own case, the calumnies were flying already in the summer of 2009, eight years after I had ceased to be an MP. Without having even made up my mind about whether to stand, I was accused of having been the puppet of – of all people – Alastair Campbell.

Mr Campbell was said by certain ill-wishers to have run my campaign in Tatton from start to finish. But I had spoken to him only three times in my life. The first was when, as Labour's director of communications, he had a reasonable interest in asking about my politics. The second was after I had been handbagged by Christine Hamilton on Knutsford Heath and he urged me to ask for a return bout (I refused). The last time was in June 1999 when he gave a speech about Kosovo justifying the British intervention and accusing the journalists who reported the war of cowardice. That was all. The Labour Party had a single liaison officer in the Tatton campaign, whose job was to report back on its progress. At one point he was heard to say: 'The agent's a Trot and the candidate's a Tory!' Although I was an unlikely stooge, the falsehoods would be recycled. That's life, as Esther might say.

A Liberal Democrat MP whose expenses were beyond reproach wrote to me, politely enough, at the height of the expenses scandal to ask whether I had employed my daughter Melissa during my time in Parliament – and if so, for how long and how much. Was this true, he wondered, or was it 'dark propaganda'? It was a fair question easily answered. She had worked on the campaign as a volunteer without being paid at all (something that I remember rather concerned her mother), but never in the House. I employed no family members from start to finish, except my younger daughter Catherine for a week of work experience, which I paid for myself. It was interesting to see, in the feverish atmosphere of the time, how falsehoods were not just recycled but newly minted.

I was also surprised to discover that my parliamentary record, which was seldom criticised at the time, was suddenly controversial. Machine politicians were clearly alarmed by the Independent threat. It might cost them otherwise safe seats. The *Mirror*'s Kevin Maguire, a Labour loyalist, said I hadn't been 'much of an MP'. I was certainly no Gladstone, but the record in fact was fairly middle-of-the-road – not as flashy as some, but certainly not as obscure as others. I had been active, as any MP would, on local issues such as the Alderley Edge bypass and the second runway of Manchester Airport. I lobbied for the local chemical and salt industries. I had served on Standards and Privileges. I had spoken up for honest politics, objecting to some provisions of the Political Parties, Elections and Referendums Act of 2000, which later experience showed to be deeply flawed. I had, I hope, brought a whiff of cordite to debates on foreign policy and Blair's wars (I was the only MP with recent front-line experience). In two debates I had defended a distinguished serving soldier from a potential charge of treason and disgraceful treatment by the Ministry of Defence police. I had led the campaign on the floor of the House for restitution to the former Far East prisoners of war: and Tony Blair, to his lasting credit, agreed in November 2000 to a measure of compensation for them, their widows and the civilian internees. I had been under pressure from constituents – many of them lifelong Tories – to break a promise and stand for a second term.

But eight years on there were nay-sayers out there trying to discredit the record who never raised their voices at the time. Again, I suppose, that's life.

There was also the press to worry about. The scrutiny is intrusive; and a lot of good people don't stand for office because they wish to protect the privacy of their families. When I opposed Eric Pickles in Brentwood in Essex in 2001, on an issue about the membership of his constituency association, the press referred to me as Ethics Man. But Ethics Man is a dangerous label to have attached to you. Even now, if I get a call from the *Daily Mirror* or the *News of the World*, my heart sinks a little. I wonder, what have they found out about me that I have myself forgotten? It is a constant, nagging, low-level worry like the wail of a distant siren.

I had a recurring dream about being back in Parliament – not just a dream, but a nightmare. I would be jolted awake by finding myself back on the little cross-bench beneath the Serjeant-at-Arms, a no man's land between the baying, jeering ranks of government and opposition. In the dream I felt I had no reason to be there, and indeed in the real world I had once despaired so much that I had fallen asleep during Prime Minister's Questions, and then walked out of it as a chronic waste of parliamentary time. If this was the best that they could do, it just didn't seem worth doing. It had no purpose but to fuel and fan the fires of party politics. What was the point of even considering a return to the House, unless it was the free parliament of a free people, instead of this hooligans' half hour?

Early in June 2009, after the Labour wipe-out in the local and European elections, I received a message from Nick Clegg, the Liberal Democrat leader. It was about the by-election in Norwich North, caused by the resignation of Ian Gibson. Mr Clegg wrote: 'It will be a by-election entirely dominated by issues of political reform and probity. Is there any way I could persuade you to consider standing in the by-election, and to do so with our support as a Lib Dem? It would be such a great opportunity to break the mould.' He suggested that the Liberal Democrats' campaigning skills and my notoriety (although he put it more kindly) would be a chance to challenge the old ways of Westminster and could make a great impact. Whether or not I was adopted would depend of course on the local party association, which would have had every right to adopt whomever it wished. The Liberal Democrats were less centrally controlled than the other parties. But like the Tories they were responding to the scandal, quite reasonably, by trying to draw their candidates from a wider pool. Nick Clegg was also reported to have approached Peter Franzen, the retiring editor of the *Eastern Daily Press*. The Conservative blogger and *Eastern Daily Press* columnist Iain Dale somehow found out about these approaches and made them public.

It was an intriguing invitation, and I did think twice about it. Nick Clegg was right about challenging the old ways of Westminster. And as it happened, I had not always been an Independent but had party political form to which I had previously confessed: in about 1960, as a student, I had been secretary of the Eastern Counties Young Liberal Federation. We had 28 members. We held meetings at the Griffin Hotel in Bury St Edmunds. I invited speakers, did the accounts and wrote up the minutes of endless debates on issues that seemed important at the time. We made no impact at all. Norwich North would be rather more in the mainstream. But the House of Commons had driven me to despair and distraction the first time around; and the Liberal Democrats already had an electable local candidate in mind. If I had intervened, it might have seemed something of – how to put it? – a stooge-like manoeuvre. And anyway it was an open seat, with no tainted MP standing for re-election. So I thanked Nick and declined.

Chapter 10

The Political Class

In February 1855 the great reformer and Quaker MP, John Bright, rose in the House of Commons and said: 'There is growing up – and no man regrets it more than I do – a bitter and angry feeling against that class which has for a long period conducted the public affairs of this country.' He was speaking at a time of economic recession and a costly foreign war in the Crimea. 'The angel of death has been abroad throughout the land,' he said, 'you can almost hear the beating of his wings.' He was later to lose his seat because of his opposition to the war.

He could have been speaking about our times rather than his. There are just a few differences between then and now. The political class was composed of landowners and manufacturers rather than the professional politicians of today. And thanks to the reporting of William Howard Russell, the British people – or at least the readers of *The Times* – were better informed about the Crimean War than the readers of any newspaper or the viewers of any TV network about today's conflicts in Iraq and Afghanistan. Today's political class appears to lack any useful grounding in history. We British are fighting our fourth Afghan war. In force levels, casualties, the ferocity of combat and probable outcomes it bears remarkable resemblances to the second, from 1878 to 1880. Our politics reflects nothing of this, and our journalism does not fill the gap. As the diktats of health and safety restrict even the war reporters, who increasingly retreat to their bunkers and ultra-safe green zones, all we are left with is rooftop journalism and a cascade of fragments masquerading as news. News as we used to know it has been laid to rest.

The third difference is that John Bright paid for his own bath plugs. He had to, because MPs were unpaid in those days, so only the wealthy could afford to seek election. I am not advocating a return to the Parliament of the plutocrats. But when MPs are elected they sign on to the seven principles of public life set out by Lord Nolan after the earlier upsurge of sleaze in Tory times. The first of these is leadership. They are supposed to set an example. So when they are paid a salary of more than two-and-a-half times the national average, and can recover all the necessary costs that go with it, they have no business claiming for items that have nothing to do with their parliamentary duties. Like duck islands. While the tides of corruption have risen and fallen over the centuries, and the Commons has never been a Parliament of saints (nor perhaps would we wish it to be), the chances of public exposure are much greater in our day, when every paperclip has to be accounted for, than they were in John Bright's. The accounts are easily copied and are there for all to see; the law has been changed to let in the light; and we know who are the honest MPs (not as many as we hoped) and who are the swindlers and sinners (a nightmarish multitude).

Even before their misdeeds came to light, there was the sense of the sort of alienation that John Bright spoke about. There seemed to be a wider breach than ever in living memory between them and us, the government and the governed, the politicians and the people. Professor Anthony King of Essex University, a magisterial authority on politics, warned of it in an influential column published shortly before the scandals surfaced: 'The deepest divide in British politics today is not between Labour and the Tories. ... It is between Britain's whole political class and the great majority of the British people. On the far side of a chasm stand politicians of all parties and their hangers-on. On the near side is almost everyone else.'[1]

Now that the MPs' secrets were out, the parties and especially their leaders had to deal with the backwash of so much public anger. The people were not storming the gates of the Palace of Westminster. The British don't do that, and this was a British revolution – no barricades, tumbrils or guillotines (except as parliamentary procedures), but a flood of angry letters to the press and to the miscreants themselves. Some of the MPs just went to ground: like the war zone reporters, they needed a fortified green zone in which to take cover. A senior Army officer with no reason to have a high opinion of them described their reactions as being like the flailings of a very sick animal.

The Conservative leader, David Cameron, showed great agility in positioning himself on the side of the seething majority. He noted that politicians were more reviled and hated than they had ever been. He said: 'We have to show that we share the public's fury', which was no easy task when so much of that fury was directed at his MPs. He called for a massive redistribution of power and a curbing of the power of the political elite and especially the Prime Minister – that is, himself, if the election went as he hoped. 'Give me less power' was an original slogan for a party leader, but it was in keeping with the spirit of the times. He said: 'We must keep a cool head and a sense of proportion. But equally, we must not let ourselves believe that a bit of technocratic tinkering here, a bit of constitutional consultation there, will do the trick.'[2]

David Cameron made another astute move. Under pressure of the crisis, he re-opened his party's candidates' list to people who shared its values but had no previous record as campaigners, or even Conservatives. If the right New Conservatives came forward – and 3,000 hopefuls volunteered – he suddenly had a selection of safe seats to offer them, recently vacated by the old guard: Macclesfield, Congleton, Totnes, Sleaford, Devizes and Gosport to name but a succulent few. The new MPs would have to take the party whip like the old ones, but the proposals came with a hint that a degree of independent thinking and voting would be tolerated from time to time. This was entirely new politics.

But the old politics still played its part. David Cameron used the scandal to purge his party, so far as possible, of elderly Members who had no place in his vision of it, but he kept his Shadow cabinet intact. Most MPs in safe seats tend to hang on to them for at least one term too many, and sometimes two. This was an easy way to send them packing. The flipping of homes was banned, of course, and substantial sums of money were repaid. But reformed front-benchers like Chris Grayling, Alan Duncan and Michael Gove all paid their dues and held on, for a while at least, to their privileged perches. They were too useful to the project to be discarded. It was an openly selective cull of the old-timers. When it was over, David Cameron admitted to some 'unfairnesses', but said he thought it was right 'to do something to make good and atone for the mistakes of the past'.[3]

The Conservatives' thought police were on high alert. When one of their own MPs, usually Alan Duncan, put his foot in his mouth on the expenses issue, he was made to retreat and retract in short order. One of the arts of politics is dodging your own side's bullets.

Next it was the turn of the Liberal Democrats. I was surprised to receive a call from Nick Clegg, who was also consulting more widely; like David Cameron he understood the gravity of the crisis and the need to reach out to Independents and other uncommitted voters. He was concerned that in certain constituencies, like Luton

South, Independents might split the anti-politics vote and prevent the election of one of his Liberal Democrats. He may have thought that I had influence with Esther Rantzen, which I did not. He called for an immediate programme of reform – not just of MPs' expenses, but of the voting system, party funding, the House of Lords, and of the Commons itself. He suggested fixed-term parliaments and a procedure to recall – meaning, to dismiss – MPs suspended under the new disciplinary procedures. 'Together, over the next hundred days, we could achieve nothing less than the total reinvention of British politics, underpinned by the fundamental principles of accountability, transparency and probity. These months would become a great moment in British political history, rather than a shabby footnote to a shameful month of scandals.'[4] He also spoke positively about Independents, although doubting whether they could accomplish much on their own. As a group, I believed, they could accomplish a great deal, especially by practising a different sort of politics, by which I mean a politics of three senses: a sense of right and wrong, common sense, and where these fail a sense of humour.

So I proposed something else to him. If his Liberal Democrats were serious about forcing the pace, they could show it by agreeing, in a few carefully chosen constituencies – not Luton South – to stand down their candidates in favour of a strong Independent seeking to unseat a tainted incumbent, whether Labour or Conservative. There was a precedent for it. They had done just that in Tatton in 1997 and in Wyre Forest in

2001. And when Richard Taylor, the Independent MP for Wyre Forest, had stood for re-election in 2005 they had not put up a candidate against him. To calm his fears, if he had any, I told Nick Clegg that this did not necessarily mean that his Liberal Democrats would have to climb on to Esther's bandwagon. (For reasons not entirely clear to me, Esther attracts more incoming fire than most.) They might prefer to help a local hero. But it would be a clear sign that they put national interest above party advantage – which of course, as the game of politics is played, would be to their party's advantage. Nick Clegg's response was cautiously positive.

I neither belonged to a political party nor was enough of an established politician to do deals with those who were in public life professionally. But I did have certain conversations with certain people. The surge of support for non-party candidates should not be squandered on frivolous causes or wasted on splitting the anti-miscreant vote. MPs who had behaved dishonestly and had not been de-selected by their parties could still be defeated, either by Independents or by the very best candidates of other parties. Some of the parties' choices were admirable, just as some Independents were decidedly odd. It was important that good candidates did not get in each others' way. And that was why I had those conversations.

Of all the parties, it was Labour who were suffering the most serious damage. They were statistically more vulnerable, because they had the most MPs. Some of their very senior figures were accused of wrong-doing, including at the time the Home Secretary, the

Transport Secretary, the Communities Secretary and the Chancellor of the Exchequer. The scandal was unfolding on their watch. Yet they seemed slow to understand its severity and the strength of public feeling. Gordon Brown said that as a son of the Manse he was appalled by the revelations, which offended his 'Presbyterian conscience'. 'I want to apologise on behalf of politicians,' he added, 'on behalf of all parties, for what has happened.' He defended the integrity of the great majority of MPs, while dismissing those who abused the expenses system as 'just a few'. It was the 'few rotten apples' theory making an inevitable comeback. The Prime Minister's personal honesty was never in doubt, as John Major's had not been, but his response seemed oddly defensive and flat-footed. Never in the field of human error had so many been described as so few. Maybe it was an effect of Downing Street's isolation. The Prime Minister's idea of a National Democratic Renewal Council sounded like something from the North Korean Politburo.

The political class had flourished till now because so much of what it did was protected by parliamentary privilege and hidden from view. It thrived on secrecy. I knew one MP who exchanged his vote for a peerage, which sounded illegal but actually was not; the House of Lords was full of Members rewarded with ermine for records of serial obedience. I knew another who owed his unwarranted promotion to high office to a friend's donation to his party. I knew a third who switched from being a rebel to a loyalist on an important vote and was rewarded by the whips with a grander House of

Commons office. Such people were infinitely *subornable*: for the right incentive – an honour, an office, the membership of a Commons committee – there is nothing they would not do, or consider doing. These were the quiet corruptions of politics as usual. Slowly and inexorably they were being forced to the surface. We are not by nature a revolutionary people. But it was only our sense of shock and embarrassment, and not any North Korean solution, that could rid us of these systemic abuses and make a fresh start possible.

There is surely a place for a handful of Independents in a House of Commons committed to that fresh start. They will all be people of wide and varied experience outside politics. It is likely that they will not be in the first flush of youth, but they will answer a real need. An electable candidate adds: 'I feel that there really could be a chance of more Independents being elected and I would like to be there to help in the face of a large number of new MPs, probably mostly Tory and insufferably young.'

The rise of the political class also connects with the issue of MPs' outside interests and second jobs – whether they should have them at all and how much they earn. A step in the right direction was taken on 1 July 2009, when MPs were obliged to declare how much they were paid, and for how many hours of work, outside their parliamentary duties. It seems to me inconsistent to complain that MPs have little experience of the real world outside politics, and then to object when they have some sort of a paid side-line. Politics is inherently insecure, and if they lose their seats they need a job to go back to. Richard Shepherd (Conservative, Aldridge Brownhills), for instance, has a directorship in his family's grocery business: 'It gives me a proper understanding of the issues faced by businesses', he says. In the same way it is not only unobjectionable, but admirable, that Desmond Swayne (Conservative, New Forest West) earns about £5,000 a year for serving as a major in the Territorial Army; that Sir Paul Beresford (Conservative, Mole Valley) is a practising dentist, especially on Sundays; and that Robert Goodwill (Conservative, Scarborough and Whitby) spends up to an hour a week digging graves on the cemetery he owns on his farm in North Yorkshire. There is something appealing about the very idea of an MP as a part-time gravedigger. (Though if a gravedigger were a part-time MP that might be harder to justify.) Frank Field (Labour, Birkenhead) felt that MPs were being sold into some sort of slavery when they had to justify every minute of the day that was not spent on parliamentary business. If they wish to write a book and can find time for it, they should do so. It should be a better book because of their public service; and an ability to communicate is actually part of the job.

An MP's office is like a small business anyway. There are staff to be employed. There is a budget to be managed and accounted for. There are clients – constituents – seeking the services of the MP, who is both the managing director and the principal case worker, at all times and in all seasons. The business is up for inspection and re-certification every four or five years; and if it fails, the entire staff, including the MP, will be swiftly out of a job. There is a further hazard: it is also usually the wholly owned subsidiary of a great corporation, the political party, and can be driven out of business because, if the branch office succeeds but the head office fails, the branch office goes down too. How long is the roll call of excellent MPs who have gone down with their sinking ships! Aside from such a catastrophic outcome, the key to success is common sense, hard work, a care for people, competence and honesty. These are not qualities possessed exclusively – or in some cases, at all – by the rising political class. I know many people outside Parliament who could do it better than a large number of those inside it. So does just about everyone else. If more of them tried it, our politics would be very much better off.

The takeover of Parliament by the political class has been a new and unwelcome phenomenon. Too many of its Members lack experience of anything but politics. A.P. Herbert had this to say about the House of half a century ago: 'You could hardly mention any subject without some Member shyly coming forward and confessing that he knows all about it, whether it is the Battle of Waterloo, the keeping of hens, the geography of Malaya or the running of a coal mine. For many years you may have maintained without much contradiction (in pubs and clubs) that all cows have five legs. But when you rise to make the same assertion in the House of Commons, you have to realise that there are 638 other

Members, each one of whom may rise, politely or not, to say that he knows more about cows than you do.'[5]

The political class has been severely knocked back, if not chastened, by the expenses scandal. That is one of its many positive outcomes. It would be a further benefit if at least some of these political insiders were to be replaced by MPs who, as in A.P. Herbert's time, knew a bit about life before they presumed to enter the House and to lay down the law for the rest of us.

Chapter 11

Downfall

The ground shook. Even without the expenses scandal, the Labour government would have had every reason to delay the election until the last possible moment in June 2010. Its poll ratings were dire. The party was deeply in debt. Its best and last hope was that some signs of economic recovery might appear towards the end of the year, and Gordon Brown could go to the country as the great helmsman, the man best qualified to steer the ship out of the storm. The 'no time for a novice' mantra would be repeated. It was a slim hope, but the only one they had.

But with the tsunami of the expenses revelations, things went from bad to worse. It was like the scene from *Richard III* where messengers rush in from all points of the compass with tidings of defeat and disaster – and, in this case, resignation. If all the ministers compromised by the scandal had stepped down because of it, Gordon Brown would have been left with only a quarter of his cabinet. As it was, he resorted to unlikely and even desperate measures, like a peerage and a place in government for the entrepreneur and TV personality Sir Alan Sugar. The peers advanced as the commoners faded from view. What with Esther and Sir Alan, politics was coming to seem like a reality TV show. At least the voters could relate to it better as viewers.

The Home Secretary Jacqui Smith, whose financial arrangements had been so questionable and whose embarrassment so acute, was first to go. Others made their own calculations about their political futures inside or outside the cabinet. Some of them were taking to the lifeboats in what appeared to be a coordinated attempt to isolate the captain on the bridge. A factious crew, indeed. It was the political equivalent of a bad day in Mogadishu – a coup that nearly succeeded but not quite. Those leaving the cabinet included Hazel Blears (Communities), James Purnell (Work and Pensions) and John Hutton (Defence). Hazel Blears flounced out spectacularly. James Purnell called for the Prime Minister to step down. John Hutton announced that he had chosen to leave politics permanently. Caroline Flint, the Europe Minister, followed them, having been denied a cabinet place in the reshuffle. The normal courtesies did not apply. In her resignation letter to Gordon Brown she wrote: 'I am extremely disappointed at your failure to have an inclusive Government. You have a two-tier Government. Your inner circle and then the remainder of Cabinet. ... Several of the women attending Cabinet – myself included – have been treated by you as little more than female window-dressing.' Was Margaret Beckett, once Foreign Secretary, also female window-dressing? After years of loyal service to the party, in government and out of it, she may have felt under-appreciated. She too was denied a seat in cabinet and returned to the back benches.

Others bowing out were Paul Murphy and Tony McNulty. Both had been touched by the expenses storm. Paul Murphy, the Welsh Secretary, had claimed £3,419 for a new plumbing system in his London house because the water was 'too hot'. Tony McNulty, the Employment Minister, had claimed almost £60,000 for a house in Harrow in which his parents lived but he did not. While denying wrong-doing he called for a reform of the system. Doug Henderson went too, the MP for Newcastle North who had charged £800 in telephone calls from his family home in a Scottish fishing village. He was 60 and believed it was time to make way for someone younger.

The attempted coup against Gordon Brown petered out. Even a thundering editorial in *The Guardian*, bulletin board of the centre left, failed to galvanise would-be plotters into action. The reason was that a new leader would not have been able to avoid calling an election; and in that election a large section of the parliamentary party, including many of the plotters, would have been wiped out. It faced extinction. Gordon Brown's government team in 2009 was much like John Major's in 1996: it appeared to be in terminal decline, but was formed up as a circular firing squad, in which no one dared pull the trigger.

The beneficiary in political terms was Lord Mandelson, twice forced to resign under Tony Blair, but now restored to office under Blair's great rival. He applied his considerable skills to persuading ministers who might have jumped ship of the merits of staying on board. 'Small earthquake, few people dead', he observed afterwards. He was now in all but name Deputy Prime Minister, with ten other ministers answerable to him, including five peers and six ministers of state. You would have to go back to Shakespeare to find so many titles in a cast of characters – and they were all combined in this one remarkable man. The Right Honourable Lord Mandelson of Foy in the county of Herefordshire and Hartlepool in the county of Durham was also Lord President of the Council, First Secretary of State, and Secretary of State for Business, Innovation and Skills. He was his party's outstanding operator: perhaps he could turn its fortunes around as he had turned his own, in a career which had all the ups and downs of a soap opera. So why should it not be a script-writer's dream and end in Number Ten? All it would take was a change in the law, which was work in progress, and he could renounce his life peerage and make a triumphal return to the Commons, feared and respected by friend and foe, via a safe seat in County Durham. The greatest come-back since Lazarus was wildly conjectured. And this was a government that was elected to office as a servant of the people, on a promise of reform, of reconnection and the devolution of power.

When the dust had settled, most of the government ministers in the greatest difficulty over their expenses had resigned or been returned to the back benches. Of those who had not, the most prominent survivor was the Chancellor, Alistair Darling, who managed to cling on to his job against the odds. This was the man to whom was entrusted the management of the nation's finances at a time of deep recession. Yet his management of his personal finances was remarkably agile. He had flipped his designated second home four times in four years (all within the rules, of course, but we know who sets the rules). When he became Chancellor he claimed a £1,004 service charge on his south London flat, at the same time as other expenses relating to his grace-and-favour residence in Downing Street. The rules are clear: an MP can claim for only one property at a time. Mr Darling admitted the error (inadvertent, of course, as all of them were) and paid back £700. MPs are supposed to set an example. Taxpayers might wonder what kind of example was set by the flipping and inadvertent over-claiming. The answer came back that the Honourable Member had made an honourable mistake. So were they all, all Honourable Members. And some of them made honourable mistakes. But very soon, under reforms proposed by the new Speaker, John Bercow, they might cease to be referred to as Honourable Members. It would be a hard habit to break, but in the light of all that had happened, it somehow made sense.

When some of the old guard of MPs came before Sir Christopher Kelly's Committee on Standards in Public Life, they tried to defend the flippers on the grounds that all they were doing was reducing their exposure to tax, as any honest citizen might do in similar circumstances. Sir Christopher gave them short shrift. He pointed out that what they were also doing was using public money to fix up one home, then another, and then, for the real enthusiasts, a third and even a fourth. He took a hostile view of it. The politics as usual crowd were in for a nasty surprise.

The first electoral returns were also coming in. The people were speaking loud and clear on the issues of the day. Labour had expected defeat, but faced a near wipe-out instead. In local elections on 4 June 2009, it was ousted from its last four county councils in England. It lost more than half of the council seats it was defending. And for the first time ever, it reversed a century of progress and slipped behind the Liberal Democrats in the opinion polls, 23 per cent to the Lib Dems' 28 per cent. Not all of its disasters were attributable to the expenses scandal. The government was unpopular anyway. But the slide was steeper because of public revulsion against the transgressions of the political class. And Labour, with so many high-profile fiddlers and flippers – a few of them, amazingly, still in office – bore the brunt of the people's anger.

The European results were even worse. Labour came third behind the Conservatives and UKIP. Its share of the vote, just 15.8 per cent, was the lowest ever recorded by a governing party. The fringe outpolled the mainstream. As a further effect of the unsettled weather and the weakening of old allegiances, Labour's collapse opened the way for the BNP to win two European seats – its first ever at parliamentary level – on only a marginal advance in its vote since the previous election. The BNP leader Nick Griffin, who took one of them, promised a transformation of British politics. The party of the extreme right, who were strong in parts of Essex, polled almost the same number of votes in the Eastern Region that I had when I stood there five years earlier as an Independent. I hoped that the voters were not the same. But the political climate was stormy and uncertain; and there was no way of knowing.

Then there was the twilight of the goats. This was from an acronym for the Government of All the Talents, men and women from outside politics who were given seats in the House of Lords in the early days of Gordon Brown's administration to broaden his range of ministers. Digby Jones, the former head of the CBI, was at Trade and Industry. Ari Darzi, a world-renowned heart surgeon, was at Health. And Mark Malloch Brown, a former UN Deputy Secretary General, was for a while an extremely effective minister at the Foreign Office. They left within two years, disillusioned by their experience of government and the quality of what Lord Jones called the 'here today gone tomorrow' politicians along-side them. Lord Malloch Brown, with more experience of statecraft than any of them, was said to have been particularly unimpressed. The only one who stayed was Admiral Lord West, a former First Sea Lord, who was the minister responsible for security. He had been the last man on deck once before, when he commanded HMS *Ardent*, sunk by the Argentine Air Force off the Falklands in 1982. It was a fair guess that he preferred the hostilities of the South Atlantic to the turf wars of Whitehall. But he stayed at the wheel.

We live under such constraints, in such straitened cir-cumstances financially, and with a politics so unsuited to so many challenges, that for the first time in our demo-cratic history it may not matter very much which party wins and which party loses in a general election. The great ideological divisions no longer exist. The parties are no longer vehicles for class interests. The arguments between them are less about principles than policies and priorities – where the burdens of taxation should fall, how to reduce waste, which publicly funded pro-grammes to save and which to cut, and so on. Politics is more a career – sometimes, as we have seen, a lucrative career – than a calling. The political class is taking over on both sides of the House. In such a situation I would argue from what I have seen, both in politics and out of it, that the usual role reversal – the turning of yesterday's opposition into today's government, and vice versa – is unlikely to make much of a difference.

Unless … unless we can liberate our MPs from the shackles of a whipping system that is working neither for them nor for us. Unless we can significantly raise their quality, and be represented by the best and the brightest, not by the most docile and compliant. Unless we can restore the function and reputation of Parliament as the true hub of the nation, in which a government's proposals are properly scrutinised and debated and decisions are taken on their merits. And unless our MPs set such an example that we can respect them as lately we have not, because by their actions they forfeited our trust in them and their confidence in themselves and each other.

Until that happens all politics will end in tears and all governments pass unmourned.

Chapter 12

Soldiers, Bankers and Swindlers

The great expenses scandal had the effect that it did, not because we had always supposed that our MPs were on the whole honest and admirable tribunes of the people. We had long harboured doubts about them. It had the effect that it did because we understood that over a period of time and for a variety of reasons our politics had become dysfunctional. Some of our elected representatives had made this happen. Others had let it happen. And the evidence of their malfeasance, when it finally came to light, not only confirmed but exceeded our worst fears and suspicions.

There was a time, as the old Soviet Union imploded, when those inside the system wished to reform it, but were reluctant to criticise it openly for fear of being seen to undermine it. So they argued that, good as it was, it could be made even better; and they came up with the idea of the 'further perfection committee'. In our case, we do not wish for further perfection committees, democratic renewal councils, an ideal state or a shining city on the hill. Nor do we even aspire to them. Politics is not a morality tale, but its dilemmas and outcomes are etched in shades of grey. Human nature being what it is, we expect our politicians to make mistakes; and, having made them, to learn from them. What we also expect in those who represent and govern us, from national to local level, is a measure of integrity and a measure of competence. No more than that – but that at least. And that is what we have been most conspicuously lacking. Our politicians have simply not been up to it. The delinquency goes back many years, possibly before my election as an MP in 1997 on an issue of medium-grade corruption. But it became undeniable in March 2003, when the British invaded Iraq in the Americans' slipstream.

It was the worst decision by a British government in my lifetime. It was a failure on every level, one of them military. I was a soldier once myself. I stay in touch. I attend military academies, medal parades and regimental homecomings. I know soldiers of all ranks and most regiments. Except at the very outset, when Saddam Hussein's weapons of mass destruction were presumed to exist by the forces sent to eliminate them, the operations in Iraq from 2003 to 2009 were universally unpopular among the military. Soldiers often relish going to war: it is after all what they are trained for. Their spirit has not been shaken, or at least not yet, by the hard grind and rising casualties of repeated tours of duty in Afghanistan. But Iraq was different. It was of dubious legality. Apart from the removal of Saddam, its objectives were unattainable by military means. Its post-war planning was not thought through. And it was insufficiently supported at home. Morale is everything. The colonel of a cavalry regiment observed that while his soldiers went off cheerfully to Afghanistan, even in the hardest of times, they returned from Iraq invariably 'down in the mouth'. A soldier posted this comment on an Army website: 'We are being asked to die for a lie with inadequate equipment. Military service is never harder and darker than when a soldier doubts the cause for which he is risking his life.'

In December 2006 I was visiting the lines of the Shaibah Logistics Base near Basra with a distinguished and thoughtful officer on his third tour of duty in Iraq. He was there at the beginning, there in the middle, and now he was there towards the end. The base was first established as an RAF airfield in 1917 in the centre of the southern Iraqi oilfields. We made no pretence then of being in Iraq to establish democracy. It was a bridge between India and Egypt and, if we could defend it by force of arms, a secure source of oil. Now as then, we were an army of occupation. That was all we were. My friend looked out from one of the watchtowers at the flares from the oilfields around us. A warning siren sounded. We heard the crump of incoming rocket fire from the Iraqi resistance. 'Now I know,' he said, 'what it must have felt like to be an officer in the Wehrmacht in occupied France in 1942.'

The expenses scandal was not a free-standing event, an exceptional phenomenon or bolt from the blue. It connected in the public mind with other and earlier failures – failures of both honesty and competence – by the same set of MPs. The debacle in Iraq was the most conspicuous of these. Sir Ken Macdonald, the former Director of Public Prosecutions, understood the political class better than most, and was dismayed by its behaviour. He put the connection between these events succinctly: 'Nobody likes to feel taken in. Enraged by the failure of a system that, if it wasn't dishonest, was surely incompetent, the scene was set for the electorate to believe the worst of all politics. ... The public are no longer prepared to be treated as outsiders peering over the gates into their own mysterious country.'[1]

The invasion of Iraq was approved by the House of Commons after a hurried debate as the troops were about to cross the start line and the missiles were being targeted on Baghdad for the campaign of shock and awe. Over two Parliaments our elected representatives spent 700 hours debating whether to kill foxes, and seven hours whether to kill people. I keep at home, as a *memento mori*, the *Hansard* version of the great debate on 18 March 2003. It reads like a postmortem on a defunct political system. Those who were present describe Tony Blair's speech to promote his war as one of the best of his career. It was a bravura performance, but shot through with falsehood about the threat posed by weapons that not only did not exist, but were believed not to exist at the time by certain senior figures inside MI6: 'Iraq has taken some steps in co-operation, but no one disputes that it is not fully co-operating. Iraq continues to deny that it has any weapons of mass destruction, although no serious intelligence service anywhere in the world believes it.' This was quite simply not true.

'In a time of universal deceit,' wrote George Orwell, 'telling the truth becomes a revolutionary act.'

Some of the most remarkable contributions were made by the Conservatives. The most serious decision a government takes is sending the armed forces to war. On this occasion the official opposition both turned up and went AWOL at the same time. They neither opposed the decision nor scrutinised it. Only thirteen of their MPs voted against it. The rest joined the rush to war with blind enthusiasm. Prominent among these were a number of senior Tories who were later to stand down under the shadow of the expenses scandal. The exception was Douglas Hogg, the man with the moat, who was one of the thirteen. The speeches of the others were linked by a common thread – a lack of judgement and good sense that extended all the way from the war in Iraq to their own financial affairs. What we did not know then, but do know now, was that even some of their expenses were dodgy dossiers.

Sir Nicholas Winterton, Conservative MP for Macclesfield, told his constituents: 'On this issue, put your trust in the Prime Minister. I firmly believe, as your Member of Parliament, that he is right.' John Maples, Conservative MP for Stratford-on-Avon: 'I believe that the Prime Minister's actions will be vindicated. ... The time has come to stop criticising and undermining him and to let him get on with the job.' And Andrew Mackay, Conservative MP for Bracknell: 'I listened carefully to what I thought was one of the Prime Minister's out-standing speeches. I was convinced and satisfied that the case had now been made.'[2]

One of these MPs made controversial tax-avoidance arrangements, another listed the RAC Club in Pall Mall for a month as his principal residence, and the third was summarily dismissed by his party leader for making unacceptable expenses claims.

All MPs will make mistakes of one sort or another, but there is no excuse for making them against plain common sense in matters large and small, like voting for an illegal war or claiming public money to pay for pot plants. In the new politics that follows the old, we have to find a place for independent-minded Members who will apply a duty of care to these judgements, whether on matters of war and peace in foreign affairs or on the pounds and pence of their expenses and allowances. It is a time for sober judgements and modest claims. We have to hold all our MPs to a certain standard of accounting. Those who get the little things right are less likely to fail on the big things. Bottom lines can be mat-ters of life and death. The independence of mind is vital.

The party system has too much to answer for. It does harm by stealth. Too many of the quiet corruptions of politics arise from it. It must not be allowed to go on wreaking havoc without reform.

Both the invasion of Iraq and the banking crisis suggested to many a degree of misgovernment and a change in the climate beyond the usual squalls and storms of public life. Professor Anthony King observed: 'Coming out of a clear blue sky, the *Daily Telegraph*'s revelations would have been shocking enough – and they have shocked even hardened cynics. But they have come out of a sky that was already overcast. Levels of distrust of politicians were at historically high levels. Decades of deceit, spin, waste, hyper-partisanship and sheer incompetence have already alienated millions of voters – possibly a majority – from the entirety of the political class. That alienation now goes both deeper and wider.'[3]

Fred the Shred may also have had something to do with it. Sir Frederick Goodwin was chief executive of the Royal Bank of Scotland during a period of rapid expansion which ended with its near-collapse in October 2008. He then retired with a £700,000 pension, a substantial part of which he later agreed to hand back. The bank was nationalised in all but name. Its fate and his pension became symbolic of the greatest banking crisis of modern times, in which fortunes were lost and reputations shredded.

The banking crisis and the expenses scandal connected with each other not as cause and effect but as what happened when greed went unchecked and institutions were regulated with so light a touch that they could go their own way towards the brink and then, with no one to restrain them, over it. At that point an individual's self-regulation, or sense of right and wrong, or whatever it was inside ourselves that we used to call conscience, also headed for the exit. There was a cultural similarity too. Banks and political parties are aggregations of competitive people whose ambition is for their tribe to outperform and outscore its rivals in the field. They will not take kindly to whistle-blowers in their midst – backbenchers or compliance officers – who warn of downturns or potential conflicts of interest. A politician heading for defeat is like an investor whose funds are on the rocks or a banker who denies the possibility of a depression. They have an interest in believing that the clouds will roll away and the blue skies will return. As a banker said during an earlier crisis: 'If I thought we were headed for depression, I couldn't get up and go to work in the morning.'

There may be a further parallel in the time frames. Those who study these mysteries, in the Bank of England and elsewhere, tell us that the average duration of a system-wide financial crisis between 1977 and 2002 was 4.3 years. That is also the average duration of a modern war – and many ancient wars too. Ratko Mladic, commander of the Bosnian Serb Army, predicted the end of the Bosnian war some months before it happened: 'All Balkan wars last four years,' he said, 'because they always have.' Along these lines, it is reasonable to predict that the restoration of trust in our politics will be at least a four-year struggle. A new Parliament will be elected with more new Members in it than at any time since 1945. But so total has been our loss of confidence that it will take them two or three years into the new Parliament to convince us that they have made a clean break with the past. The original Augean stables were cleaned out only when Hercules diverted two rivers through them.

The Commons has a river running past it rather than through it; and what is needed in this case is a Herculean process of deep fumigation from floor to roof. The expenses scandal has been so far-reaching, and the MPs themselves have properly been made so crestfallen by it, that at least initially they accepted what they had previously resisted, which was a measure of outside regulation. They no longer trusted themselves to put their own House in order, but they trusted no one else either. So they ended up in a mid-river predicament, buffeted by tides and currents but with no one at the helm.

Alan Johnson, MP for Hull West and a candidate-in-waiting for the Labour leadership, observed: 'As we stand marooned on Duck Island, it feels as if we'll wait some time before a return ticket to the human race arrives.' In the same column he declared that politics can be cleaned up 'without the help of irritating, self-righteous men in white suits'.[4] I am not sure who he was referring to, but if he meant me, I have known worse. I was once even called an old bomb dodger. So a ministerial put-down was like water off a duck's back on its way to the duck island.

It was during the end of my time on Standards and Privileges that I came to the conclusion that the House of Commons was incapable of regulating itself. This was during the investigation of a complaint against a senior MP for using his allowances improperly. The Commissioner, Elizabeth Filkin, upheld a part of the complaint. I know for certain that one of the other MPs on the Committee agreed with her, but when it came to a decision he voted the other way. Others did the same. It was a party political stitch-up.

Despite this, most Committee members believed that the system, although imperfect, was working reasonably well and should be continued – until the storm of the expenses scandal broke over it. At that point everything changed. The Commons was compelled to adopt external regulation which for the first time ever would challenge and diminish its sovereignty, but to the least extent that it could get away with. It was potentially a major constitutional change – more of a break with the past even than the introduction of universal suffrage. And so great was the need for it that it was adopted without a referendum, a vote of no confidence or even a prolonged debate. The rush to remodel was unstoppable, and the debate took just three days. Sir George Young, chairman of the Standards and Privileges Committee, said: 'We are on a journey with destination unknown.'[5] Gordon Brown called it the biggest reform ever seen in

Parliament: 'I am determined that it is cleaned up in such a way that we can say to the people of this country: "We listened, we heard, we knew something was wrong, we have now dealt with it."'[6] It took him a long time to get there, but he finally conceded that the House had been operating in a moral vacuum. It had been apparent to some of us since the Bernie Ecclestone affair soon after Labour took office. That vacuum would now be filled in theory by an outside agency. But, as would soon become clear, the House still preferred an empty space to an effective regulator.

Chapter 13

Afghanistan – A Study in Contrasts

The expenses scandal coincided with an upsurge in the fighting and the casualties in Afghanistan. British troops were involved in their most intensive combat since the Korean War. In the first ten days of July 2009, during Operation Panther's Claw, fifteen British soldiers were killed in Helmand Province, including Lieutenant-Colonel Rupert Thorneloe, Commanding Officer of the 1st Battalion the Welsh Guards. Fifty-seven were wounded in action during the same operation, the highest level of battlefield casualties so far. Questions arose about the suitability of some of the patrol vehicles which had been used in Afghanistan, especially the lightly armoured Snatch Land Rovers, and the chronic shortage of airlift, especially helicopters. The troop transport air bridge between RAF Brize Norton and Kandahar, consisting of three elderly Lockheed Tristars, was also vulnerable to breakdown. Force levels, objectives and logistics have to be within reach of each other, which these were not. The armed forces were paying the price, sometimes with their lives, for years of cost-cutting and a procurement policy of 'just enough just in time', which only too often translated into 'not enough and far too late'. The modern soldier knows what is going on and what lies ahead. There are not many smiles to be seen on those outgoing flights from Brize Norton; the soldiers are lost in their own thoughts. As if they needed reminding, the aircraft are fitted with racks for returning stretcher cases. United Nations flights are much the same; and unless you are a visiting politician, you can hardly fly on what we used to know as Maybe Airways without wondering whether you will come back dead or alive, and what horrors you may suffer and see in the meantime.

From the soldiers' website, the Army Rumour Service: 'What can be done to purge Parliament of these dishonest people?'[1] The contrast between the hardships endured by the soldiers and the privileges enjoyed by the politicians was in plain view, especially by the military, all the way from Helmand Province to Westminster.

When the number of soldiers killed rose to 184, the death toll in Afghanistan exceeded that in Iraq. 9 Platoon of C Company 2 Rifles lost five men killed and five wounded in a single ambush. The Commanding Officer, Lieutenant-Colonel Robert Thomson, said: 'It has been a grim day here in Sangin but at the end of the day, as we prayed for our fellow riflemen who have given their lives in the service of their country, and for the good of the Afghan people, the Bugle Major sounded the advance and it would have been heard right across the valley as the sun slipped behind the ridge. We turned to our right, saluted the fallen and the wounded, picked up our rifles and returned to the rampart. I sensed every rifleman killed in action today standing behind us as we returned to our posts, and we all knew that each of those riflemen would have wanted us to "crack on".' His words were read out at a service for the fallen at the main base in Camp Bastion.

From the sailors' website, Rum Ration: 'While you all were fiddling your expenses, our men were dying from want of helicopters.'[2]

The Defence Secretary at the time was Bob Ainsworth, Labour MP for Coventry North East, a former Deputy Chief Whip, and ranking no higher than 21 out of 23 in the cabinet's order of seniority. He said: 'Let us be under no illusion. The situation in Afghanistan is serious, and not yet decided. The way forward is hard and dangerous. More lives will be lost and our resolve will be tested.'[3] Like all of the government's previous Defence Secretaries, and indeed all of its ministers from start to finish, Mr Ainsworth had no military experience, although he had previously been Minister for the Armed Forces. At a time of military emergency there were many, both inside and outside the armed forces, who wondered whether he was up to it. He answered:

'I don't try to pretend that I am cleverer than a general or the Chief of Defence Staff. But I can bring something else, a knowledge and understanding of Parliament and of civilian life.'[4] One of his junior ministers had a back-bench record of hostility to the Army, which worried the generals considerably when he was promoted. From 2002 onwards, the operations in this most hazardous and historic of war zones were ordered and directed by politicians whose military experience amounted to the square root of nothing: they had not themselves worn the uniform, understood soldiering or done a single day of it. They had no knowledge especially of its hard and dark side. They sent out others to put their lives on the line, but their own were lived in safety and comfort, on fitted furniture and in medal-free zones.

Bob Ainsworth claimed nearly £6,000 for the redecoration of his second home. His claims included £2,225 for a corner sofa, which the Fees Office rejected. He wrote: 'If you feel this is excessive, can I say that due to the size and layout of the room, a normal three piece suite will not fit. This "corner group" fits perfectly and maximises the space.'

Geoff Hoon was the longest-serving of New Labour's six Defence Secretaries, a wastefully high rate of turn-over. He held the post from 1999 to 2005, a period that included the invasion of Iraq and the beginning of the open-ended commitment to Afghanistan. For a reason that was never entirely clear, he was uniquely unpopular among the armed forces, who invented a disparaging acronym for him. It was his successor John Reid and not Hoon himself who visited Kabul in April 2006 and was quoted by Reuters as saying: 'We would be perfectly happy to leave in three years' time without firing one shot.' Some infantry battalions in the fighting season, like the 1st Royal Anglians, would fire a million in their six-month tour of duty. More than twelve million were fired in those three years, including 150,000 from attack helicopters. Reid's remarks were thrown back at him. He always claimed he was misrepresented: it was a wish or hope and not a prediction. Even as a wish or hope it was wide of the mark; but he was well respected by the military: he could talk their talk, and it was the view of some senior officers that if he had chosen to be a soldier rather than a politician he would have made an excellent regimental sergeant major. Instead of which he was Secretary of State. By then Geoff Hoon was a Foreign Office minister with responsibility for Afghanistan. The casualties were rising and the costs of the war were being, quite literally, brought home every week to RAF Lyneham in flag-draped coffins and saluted as they passed through the town of Wootton Bassett. He said: 'We always anticipated that the resistance, particularly of the criminal and terrorist elements in the south, would be one of the most difficult problems, so it is not surprising that we are facing these kinds of attacks in the south. That was always anticipated and it was always planned for.'[5]

Geoff Hoon was a man of substance; he flipped his homes and took advantage of a loophole which allowed him to avoid paying capital gains tax on one of his properties. He said that he saw no reason to pay it back. He did, however, repay £384 for costs incurred on his constituency home in Derbyshire after he had flipped his second home to London. He claimed the maximum of £400 for food.

Lieutenant-Colonel Stuart Tootal, former Commanding Officer of 3 Para, recalled some hard fighting in 2006 when his battle group lost three dead and eighteen wounded in Helmand in one day: 'After months of near continuous close combat, we had many days like it, but the next day people always climbed back into poorly protected vehicles or overworked helicopters and continued to hold positions with too few troops. Led by their commanders, they went back into battle without complaint and with a quiet determination to succeed; it is what British soldiers do. ... The shining example of decisiveness and conviction needs to be reflected at the highest echelons of the MoD and government.'[6] Colonel Tootal was one of many front-line commanders who had pleaded in vain for more helicopters.

A story goes the rounds in the Army of a senior minister who was inspecting the troops, at a suitably safe distance from the front line, in one of Tony Blair's optional wars. To break an awkward silence an intrepid squaddie from a Scottish regiment asked him: 'Excuse me, sir, but how much do you know about soldiering?' 'Not very much,'

*said the minister, 'but how much do you know about poli-
tics?' 'Not very much either,' replied the squaddie, 'but
my friends tell me that I am a very good liar!'*

Politicians are ill at ease with outspoken soldiers. They do
not like to be challenged by men in uniform. They prefer
their generals to be quiet, deferential ticks-in-the-boxes
types who serve loyally, collect the honours that go with
the rank and then discreetly retire. General Sir Richard
Dannatt, Chief of the General Staff during this period,
was not cast in that mould. Shortly after taking office
in 2006 he had publicly recommended the withdrawal
of his troops from Iraq 'sometime soon'. He was right
of course, but he was often misquoted and misunder-
stood, and his honesty led to calls for his dismissal. He
championed his soldiers' rights and welfare. He broke
down the barriers between them and civil society with a
series of initiatives, including homecoming parades for
battalions returning from Iraq and Afghanistan. People
turned out in great numbers to cheer the troops and to
support the service charities. 'They made our soldiers
march ten feet tall', he said. General Dannatt did not
shoot from the hip. His interventions were deliberate
and calculated, and usually made after an unsatisfactory
meeting with a politician. His soldiers and their families
depended on him. On the deployment in Afghanistan he
said: 'We didn't know what we didn't know, and after we
got there we knew a lot less.'[7] In July 2009 he briefed a
group of MPs that the Army needed 2,000 more troops
in Helmand Province to hold the ground it had won.

He was allowed only 700 as a stop-gap measure. A government minister accused him, anonymously as always, of meddling in politics and of overstepping the line yet again. Lord Foulkes, a hard-to-admire politician from the ranks of Scottish Labour, dared to accuse General Dannatt, who was the soldiers' hero, of 'giving succour' to their enemies in the Taliban. For his farewell battlefield tour in Helmand, he had to borrow an American Black Hawk helicopter: 'Self-evidently,' he said, 'I have to move in an American helicopter because there is not a British helicopter.' At that point his critics in the government accused him of playing 'helicopter politics', because the shortage of helicopters was rightly a big issue, but by then he was probably past caring about politicians or anything but the Army. He was about to retire and – in the long British tradition of those who challenge the Executive – to be despatched to the Tower of London, but as its Constable.

History tells us that we have been here before. Mesopotamia (now Iraq) was another British military graveyard. Kipling wrote these lines about it in 1917:

> *Our dead shall not return to us while Day and*
> *Night divide –*
> *Never while the bars of sunset hold.*
> *But the idle-minded overlings who quibbled while*
> *they died,*
> *Shall they thrust for high employments as of old?*[8]

In 2006 the then Prime Minister Tony Blair promised the armed forces everything they needed to take on the Taliban.

Three years later, in May 2009, Lieutenant Mark Evison of the Welsh Guards died of his wounds in Helmand Province. He had a reputation as an outstanding young officer. He had served as a platoon commander in Afghanistan for less than a month, which was time enough to get to know the shortages. He wrote in his journal: 'I have a lack of radios, water, food and medical equipment. This with manpower is what these missions lack. Injuries will be sustained which I will not be able to treat and deaths could occur which could have been stopped. We are walking on a tightrope and from what it seems here are likely to fail.'[9]

After the death of his only son John with the Irish Guards in the Battle of Loos, Kipling wrote his 'Epitaphs of the War':

If any question why we died,
Tell them, because our fathers lied.[10]

The rain lifted. The crowds cheered. Bayonets were fixed and regimental colours were flown. On 17 July 2009 the bands of the Parachute Regiment and the Army Air Corps led the parade as more than 700 men of 16 Air Assault Brigade marched through Colchester, exercising the freedom of the town which had been awarded to them eighteen months earlier. They had been too busy in Helmand Province to do it before. Colchester is a garrison town, and because of the Paras' casualties and multiple deployments this was in some ways the most heartfelt homecoming of them all. The Army was no longer behind the wire, but part of the wider community. The Brigade, including 2 and 3 Para and their many supporting units, had returned from its second tour of duty in Afghanistan, only eighteen months after its first. A third was already planned. That was an effect of overstretch: too few were being deployed too soon to do too much and with insufficient back-up. The costs had been high: 31 men killed and 197 wounded in just six months in 2008, with many others patched up in the field and soldiering on. Other casualties, from the unseen injuries of the mind, would not be known for years. One of the dead was Trooper James Munday of D Squadron the Household Cavalry Regiment, which provided armoured reconnaissance for the Paras. He died on 15 October 2008, two weeks before the end of his tour of duty. For the bereaved, the fall-out of the scandal was very personal.

'I hope our Government will stop feathering its own nest and provide our guys with the best equipment they can because they deserve it,' said Trooper Munday's mother Caroline, after his inquest in Warwickshire.[11]

To a politician, a luxury is a plasma TV; an emergency is a falling-out with the constituency association; and a fallen comrade is an MP of the same party who, having been exposed as a flipper and swindler, has finally been forced into retirement.

To a soldier, a luxury is a bucket of water; an emergency is an all-arms Taliban assault on a forward operating base; and a fallen comrade is a friend who has fought alongside him and saved his life, and whose remains he is trying to extract from the wreck of a blown up armoured patrol vehicle.

Here is an evidence-based story from the House of Commons. An MP tells his regional whip that, on grounds of conscience, he cannot vote for his party's policy of 42 days' detention without charge. The whip warns him of the political consequences and reminds him that he was elected not because of his conscience but because of his party. He is therefore obliged to vote with his Honourable Friends. The MP falls into line and obediently troops through the Aye lobby. He and the whip then celebrate their victory in a manner paid for by the benevolent taxpayer through the flow of petty cash.

And here is a Parachute Regiment corporal's story, direct from the Helmand battlefield, real-world and verbatim: 'When we move, we create a dust cloud that can be seen for 40 kilometres. There is no safety bubble. ... A soldier died. The platoon commander asked me if I was all right. I told him that I wanted to be alone. And then we cracked on.'

Chapter 14

An Act of Sabotage

The restoration of confidence in our elected representatives was more a matter for them than for anyone else. They had a professional interest in winning it back. But on past experience they could not be relied on to do that on their own. And so was born their new regulator, the Independent Parliamentary Standards Authority – its provisional title, with the extent of its powers not yet agreed and the details still being argued around the drawing board. In theory at least it would be less of a poodle and more of a Doberman than the watchdog it replaced. It would oversee and regulate MPs' expense claims. It would enforce the new and tighter rules – still being drawn up by the Kelly Committee – on what could and could not be claimed. A Commissioner for Parliamentary Investigations would report to the Authority, which would recommend to the House the suspension or expulsion of erring MPs. The most serious cases would be referred to the police. It would create a new criminal offence for MPs of 'knowingly providing false or misleading information in a claim for an allowance', punishable by up to a year in prison or an unlimited fine. An MP who failed to register an interest, or broke the rules on paid advocacy, would be fined up to £5,000. The plans for the new regulator sounded impressive, until the MPs got at them.

The idea of the sovereignty of Parliament is as old as our unwritten constitution. It means that Parliament is the paramount institution; that the laws it passes can be interpreted but not overturned or judicially reviewed in the courts; that they are not binding on future Parliaments, but can be repealed or amended as times change; that it is the defender of the liberties of the people against abuses of power, originally by the Crown but now by any other over-reaching agent of authority. The irony of the Duck Island Parliament was that the Members of the House, instead of defending the people, were seen to be enriching themselves at the people's expense. It was not the MPs who needed protection from the people, as a few of them supposed, for the people under great provocation behaved with remarkable restraint. It was the people who needed protection from the MPs. So this was more than the failure of a system. It was a real constitutional crisis. And the new legislation might as well have been entitled 'The Dangerous MPs Act'.

If the MPs objected to the changes – and many of them did – they had only themselves to blame. It was their own misconduct that had made these changes necessary. In his evidence to the Kelly Committee the political journalist Peter Oborne observed: 'We are on the verge of abandoning the ancient doctrine of parliamentary sovereignty and replacing it with a system which effectively means legal control over the legislature. The idea that parliament is the highest court in Britain may be smashed. ... All of my personal sympathies and prejudices are with parliamentary sovereignty. However everything I have witnessed as a parliamentary reporter over the last decade points towards the bankruptcy of the old system.'[1]

The Independent Parliamentary Standards Authority (IPSA) was a statutory halfway house. It had to be more genuinely independent of the Commons than the system it replaced, yet not so far outside the House as to become a rival and alternative centre of power. Frictions were inevitable. It had to police the Commons and yet to work with it. The IPSA would consist of five members including a chairman, 'To be appointed by Her Majesty on an address of the House of Commons'. At least one of the five must have held high judicial office, one must be a qualified auditor and one must have had parliamentary experience, but not within the previous five years. Each one of those appointments would be scrutinised by MPs with more rigour than they had ever used to scrutinise each other, even in the darkest days on Standards and Privileges. Entire careers depended on it.

Parliament kept control, in the sense that either the chairman or an ordinary member could be removed from office 'On an address of both Houses of Parliament'. But it lost control, in the sense that the regulatory system would be more powerful and (in the Bill's original draft) proceedings in Parliament could be used as evidence in criminal prosecutions. This set off alarm bells among the traditionalists. Malcolm Jack, the Clerk who oversees the rules of the House, warned that: 'This could have a chilling effect on the freedom of speech of Members and of witnesses before committees and would hamper the ability of House officials to give advice to Members.' Almost by definition MPs lead privileged lives. The flag of privilege is one to which they will rally. But as Dr Tony Wright MP pointed out, who was once a professor of politics: 'The problem with parliamentary privilege is that nobody, apart from the Clerk of the House, quite knows what it means.'[2]

The only part of privilege that really matters has nothing to do with maces, wigs, swords and other parliamentary paraphernalia: it is the right of MPs to speak freely in the House without the threat of being dragged through the libel courts for doing so. In every other respect they should be subject to the same laws, and the same penalties for breaking them, as every other citizen in the country. The Parliamentary Standards Bill was a faltering attempt to drag them in that direction.

A seemingly arcane issue was of high importance. To put it more colloquially: the sheriff was getting access to the saloon bar, and the regulars in the saloon bar were fighting back. Decisions taken in just a few days would shape the future of Parliament for many years.

The Clerk's warnings were heeded. At the end of the debate the government suffered one of its rare defeats, on the issue of the use of Commons proceedings as possible evidence in a criminal prosecution. Two Labour loyalists and former ministers, John Reid and Margaret Beckett, were among those opposing the controversial clause. 'The mood these past few days has been different,' wrote the Tory MP Douglas Carswell, 'decisions are being made, not rubber-stamped, in the chamber. This is a glimpse of what the new Commons could be.'

The government also dropped its proposal to have the MPs' code of conduct enshrined in law. This made for a good soundbite but was unworkable in practice. To measure MPs by their performance – how many questions tabled, how many speeches made, how many hours a week of constituency surgeries – may have seemed fine in theory, but would have opened the door to mischievous litigation. Something like this had happened even under the old system. A political opponent would write to the Commissioner for Standards complaining that Jeremiah Jobsworth, MP for Barsetshire Central, had disappeared from the radar completely, was seldom seen in the House and doing nothing for his constituents. The complaint would generate some anti-Jobsworth headlines in the local press, as it was intended to. But the Commissioner always rejected it. Diligence was not one of the seven principles of public life. As the rules were written, all that an MP had to do after being elected was to take the oath of office on the floor of the House. He could then spend the next four years on a Caribbean beach without the voters holding him to account – except of course at the next election. And this, or something like it, had happened quite regularly. One of the MPs disgraced by the expenses scandal had disappeared from view to nurse her sorrows. Her constituents were unrepresented for more than a year but there was nothing they could do about it. In the previous Parliament another MP had so completely disappeared from view that his constituents and even his local paper couldn't find him; again there was nothing that they could do about it. Any statutory attempt to get MPs to work harder would fall foul of the grift and graft of party politics.

The first draft of the Bill to establish the IPSA was not perfect – no Bill is – but seemed to me to strike a reasonable balance between the rights and duties of MPs. Mainly it was the amendments that did the damage. And even if it had passed without them, there had to be the most serious doubt about the role of the House of Commons in choosing its regulator. It was as if a defendant had the right to select his judge. The Speaker and his special committee would decide on the appointment of the five Commissioners, and the whole House could – in theory at least – remove them. Had we not been this way before with Elizabeth Filkin? The House invited her in, then threw her out. The more principled MPs were aware at the time that it was a disgraceful episode with far-reaching consequences. In 2002 Dr Tony Wright MP gave evidence to the Committee on Standards in Public Life: 'The Filkin affair was damaging ... it has set back a process of reform and the restoration of reputations a good deal. And it has of course revealed ... some of the shortcomings in how we do these things.' Charles Clarke MP, then chairman of the Labour Party, said: 'I think it is a relatively uncontroversial statement that the events that took place around that time gave an impression publicly that we were not addressing these things as we needed to.' Paul Tyler MP spoke for the Liberal Democrats: 'If we do not get it right, we may be in the last chance saloon for self-regulation.' And Alex Salmond MP for the Scottish National Party: 'I do not have any confidence in any aspect of self-regulation through the Standards Committee ... the evidence against that type of self-regulation is overwhelming.'[3]

Now, against all the evidence of past malpractice, MPs were insisting on the right to pick their regulator and make the same mistakes all over again. In her evidence to the Kelly Committee, Elizabeth Filkin pointed out the error of their ways: 'That method of appointment has been shown to be wanting. It is shot. You cannot use it again, however good the people who are now in those roles are.'[4] She also suggested, since she had personal experience of the quiet corruptions of the honours system, that there should be no expectation of preferment or honours for the members of the Authority. If they were looking for a knighthood or damehood, they were applying for the wrong job. She would now be Dame Elizabeth if, as Commissioner for Standards, she had been willing to believe the assurances of errant MPs. Elizabeth Filkin had been a personal witness of Parliament's inability to police itself. She had seen the fleeting consequences of an MP's suspension: 'Yes, people got slightly bad press in their home town but if you look at the careers of people after that, people who have been through being expelled, then they become chairs of Select Committees. It is amazing.'[5] She favoured tough statutory regulation and the abolition of the Committee on Standards and Privileges.

Much of this was the revisiting of old battlefields. Elizabeth Filkin's removal from office in February 2002 can now be seen as a pivotal event in the whole shabby spectacle of the MPs' abuse of their allowances. Indeed I know some good and decent MPs – yes, they do exist – who trace the expenses scandal back to that moment. From that point on, the snouts were in the trough. MPs could claim what they wanted and get away with it. The allowances were not only generous to a fault, but claimed and paid in secret. There was no reason why anyone would know. If no one would know, just about anything could be claimed. That was how it worked. Parliamentary privilege protected the cash machine. Would the Honourable Member like to have his grocery bills paid for? Why of course, up to £400 a month, with no questions asked and no receipts required. A plasma

TV set? No problem at all. Or a fitted kitchen? The very best that John Lewis could provide, so long as it wasn't obviously extravagant. That was why they usually beat a path to John Lewis and not to Harrods.

If any misdemeanour came to light, the evidence was usually anecdotal; or if the witness wished for anonymity, the rules did not allow it. The Commissioner would be unlikely to uphold a complaint; and even if he did, the errant MPs could rely on their friends on the Committee on Standards and Privileges to take a lenient view. Tea room conversations could influence the outcome. Those on the Committee who defended the indefensible – some of them, alas, still serving MPs – bore a heavy responsibility for the consequences. Senior MPs who were the subject of a complaint enjoyed a special protection, because they had more to lose if censured – and I heard this argued many times in Committee Room 13 – so the case against them was required to clear a higher hurdle of probability. They were also of course more influential and had friends in high places, including on the Committee on Standards and Privileges. And so the Commons sleep-walked into scandal. Those who made the laws for others enjoyed the advantage, if accused of breaking their own rules, of being above the law themselves.

In theory it could happen again, especially after the Parliamentary Standards Bill's rough passage through Parliament, shedding important clauses on the way. The old system of semi-detached regulation can still make a comeback under the new regulations. The five Commissioners who run the Authority must not expect to be popular. Their rulings may be challenged and – this is the ambiguity of it – might even be overturned. The House of Commons will surely come to regret its rushed, back-tracking amendments, especially the dropping of the clause to allow the proceedings of the House to be used as evidence in court. Suppose MPs could be hired like taxi-drivers (and in one notorious case it actually happened). Suppose that they were to promote a particular financial interest on the floor of the House or one of its committees. Suppose then that they sought to benefit financially from their interventions, by collecting their fees, or fares, from the special interest that hired them. Then their words in the House could not be used as evidence against them. The case might be impossible to prove. It was one thing to invoke parliamentary privilege to save MPs from being sued for libel. It was quite another to do so to prevent them from being charged with or convicted of corruption; they should be open to the same rules of evidence as every other citizen. Equality before the law is one of our most basic principles. It should apply to MPs too, especially in the light of recent events. By defending their privileges the diehards of the old guard, even now, were seeking protections under the law which anyone else who was charged with fraud could not enjoy.

And the old guard did fight back. Lord Strathclyde, the Conservatives' leader in the Lords, declared: 'The basic freedoms of Parliament are being casually thrown into doubt.'[6] As amendment after amendment was hastily debated in the Commons, David Heathcoat-Amory (Conservative, Wells) said: 'We are trying to improve a Bill that is irretrievably broken.' Sir Patrick Cormack (Conservative, South Staffordshire) spoke of the seething anger of the House. 'This is a monstrous Bill,' he said, 'which has been pushed through with indecent haste. ... This is a black day for Parliament.'[7]

There was an obvious answer to this. Was not the publication of MPs' expenses also a black day for Parliament? And the redaction of them an even blacker day? The Parliamentary Standards Bill would not have happened without them. But still the last-ditch defenders resisted it.

The House of Lords was unremittingly hostile. Its Select Committee on the Constitution objected to parts of the new measure in principle, but above all to its being railroaded through Parliament at such speed. 'The Bill will ... have to be substantially recast. To do so under an accelerated passage is in our view wholly unacceptable given the questions of constitutional principle and detail that it raises. ... There is an undoubted need to restore public confidence in the parliamentary system. It is not, however, clear that this cobbled together Bill rushed through Parliament will help rebuild public trust. On the contrary, if Parliament cannot be seen to be scrutinising proposals with the thoroughness they deserve, public confidence in Parliamentarians is likely to be further undermined.'[8]

At this point something extraordinary happened. It was not the Commons but the Lords that led the defence of MPs' rights, and sought to limit as far as possible the powers of the external regulator. Many life peers had been MPs themselves – the Lords was their retirement home – and they looked on the transgressions of the new generation as a benevolent uncle might on an errant nephew. It had not been like that in their time. They made it their business to try to save the Commons from itself. The charge was led not by the ex-MPs but by the surviving hereditary peers. They understood privilege, because they were born to it. No one understood it better than Michael, 7th Earl of Onslow, who was a public figure in his own right as a flamboyant Tory, and the only hereditary peer ever to appear on *Have I Got News For You*. His speech in the Lords was remarkable even by his standards: 'All my House of Commons friends tell me that the morale of that House is absolutely terrible. They are shell shocked and shattered. They have been spat on by their constituents and ghastly things have happened to them. ... It is up to us to try to give the House of Commons back its self-respect. In doing so, we must stick up for Members' rights, because they are at the moment feeling a little frightened so to do.'[9]

The political class ganged up against the Bill. If it had been a proposal to regulate any other profession – and they had regulated other professions – they would surely have written in safeguards against every possible abuse of power and privilege. But this was not a Bill to regulate anyone else: it was a Bill to regulate themselves. So they drew its teeth. They not only threw out the clause to allow an MP's actions in the House to be used in a court of law. They removed a section of the Bill that would have made it an offence for an MP to fail to comply with the register of Members' interests to be maintained by the newly established IPSA. They watered down the provisions on paid advocacy. They manoeuvred it onto a middle ground where, if it threatens their peace of mind, they may eventually be able to capture it. They did what they always do, given half a chance, which is to propose one set of rules for everyone else and another for themselves. The shipwreck of the Bill received little attention. The scandal by this time was off the front pages, and MPs may have felt they could treat it as a summer storm that had blown over. But it had not blown over. And attempts to emasculate the new Authority could do them great damage in the long term. After all that had happened, and the MPs themselves and their friends in the Lords had got at it, it had to be very much more than an outsourced Fees Office. One of the lessons of history, unfortunately, is that we don't learn the lessons of history.

The Parliamentary Standards Bill was rushed through Parliament, from start to finish, in less than a month. It was not so much a measure as a half-measure. By the time they were through with it, the Lords and Commons had stripped the Authority of the power to discipline MPs or even to require them to pay back money improperly claimed. The MPs would continue to deal with their own, as they always had, through the uncertain instrument of the Committee on Standards and Privileges. The Honourable Members and Noble Lords responded to the crisis with a unique, and very parliamentary, blend of defiance and contrition. The Justice Secretary Jack Straw, who finagled the Act onto the statute book, spoke eloquently of the shame of their expenses claims: 'It has been very damaging,' he said, 'without any question, profoundly damaging. It has made the whole of politics feel unclean. ... It has been terrible. I say it has been terrible not least because we have prided ourselves on high standards in British politics.'[10] And yet these same MPs, dishonoured and discredited, stood in the last ditch to emasculate the Bill, to defend their privileges, and to save themselves from external scrutiny. The IPSA that survived the Bill was, as the Texans say, all hat and no cattle. It was a return in all but name to self-regulation. The passage of the Bill was a *tour de farce* and a victory for the old politics over the new.

Sir Christopher Kelly described the Bill as 'transitional' – a clear indication that he was not satisfied with it and regarded the new arrangements as work in progress. At the end of his Committee's public hearings he had a vivid reminder of the failure of the old system which, however discredited, sat uneasily alongside the new one. The hitherto invisible Parliamentary Commissioner for

Standards, Mr John Lyon, was put under pressure to give evidence, and finally agreed to do so. It may be remembered that it was he who, at the outset of the scandal, had initially declined to investigate Jacqui Smith's use of the Alternative Costs Allowance. Sir Christopher asked him whether it might have been a good idea to investigate abuses without waiting for a formal complaint. Might that have prevented the MPs' abuse of their expenses?

'I don't want to get into might-have-beens', said Mr Lyon.

'I do', replied Sir Christopher rather sharply. And one of his colleagues, Elizabeth Vallance, observed: 'You have carved out quite a limited view of your own role.'[11] Mr Lyon testified that he had not encountered political interference. That had not been Elizabeth Filkin's experience when she was Commissioner for Standards and found herself under the most relentless pressure. But they were different characters: one of them upset the political class and the other one did not.

The people protested. The politicians resisted. We are now at a make-or-break point. Some good may yet come of the half-measures that limped onto the statute book after the MPs had hacked away at this latest attempt to bring them into line. The effectiveness of the new regime depends on the quality and independence – I would even say, the bloody-mindedness – of the IPSA's Commissioners and especially its chairman, and their determination to save themselves from the fate of regulatory capture. It depends on Sir Christopher Kelly and his Committee making clear their dissatisfaction with the legislative ruin of the Parliamentary Standards Bill. It depends on the willingness of MPs to abide by the decisions of the new Authority, however inadequate its mandate. It depends on the outcome of the very first case in which an MP, charged with a breach of the rules, faces the judgement of the Committee on Standards and Privileges and ultimately of the House. If the MPs fail the test again, as so often in the past, then it will be for the people to judge them through the ballot box and for the Kelly Committee to demand a more effective Authority to hold them to account. Failing that, the House of Commons will be condemned to a future like its past, as a house of ill-repute and an occasional chamber of horrors, or as the old Puritan Wentworth put it, 'a very school of flattery and dissimulation'. We have indeed been there before.

Chapter 15

A Democratic Blueprint

We are where we are because of politicians who let us down. They betrayed us and embarrassed us. It did not say much for our judgement that they had persuaded us to vote for them, sometimes repeatedly; but now the truth was out and we knew who they were. They also let themselves down, and each other. They said things like, 'I had no idea what my colleagues were up to'. Their colleagues said the same of them. They started to wonder what name historians would attach to the Parliament of 2005 to 2010. Sir Patrick Cormack observed: 'I fear it may go down as the tarnished or tainted Parliament. Among those of us who have sat in this Chamber in the past few weeks, it will certainly go down as the depressed Parliament.'[1]

We now have to put in place a system in which these depressions and betrayals are no longer possible, our politics has a chance of becoming more honest, and our MPs can retrieve the respect and the trust of the people. It may be a long haul. But wherever we go to has to be better than where we have come from, a House that is tarnished and tainted even in the eyes of many who sit in it. And the renewal has to start now with a parallel process of clearing out the old and building something better in its place.

The scandals have opened up a national debate on constitutional changes, many of them long overdue. The House has a long history of rushing through legislation in haste – from anti-terrorist laws to the Dangerous Dogs Act – that it later repents at leisure. I think we should draw a distinction here between grand plans for reform on the one hand, like a People's Assembly or a Bill of Rights, and, on the other, short- and medium-term proposals which result in the election of new MPs of a generally higher calibre, and observing higher standards, than the old ones they replace. Then it will be the time for a new, improved House to consider such issues as fixed-term parliaments, a three-term limit on the length of MPs' service, and a smaller House with perhaps 400 Members instead of the present 646, as well as the still only half-grasped nettle of the reform of the House of Lords. The Lords have had scandals of their own; and the danger of an all-elected Upper House is that the parties will tighten their grip on it and it will replicate the very worst of the House of Commons. In the New Labour years, and even before them, we have suffered enough from one rubber-stamp assembly not to want another. So our immediate concern is with the Commons. I suggest six measures of reform, or at least of doing things differently – and an apology.

1. Adoption in full of the Kelly Committee's proposals on MPs' expenses and allowances

The Committee on Standards in Public Life first wished to look at the expenses issue after the Derek Conway affair in January 2008, when the Conservative MP for Old Bexley and Sidcup was found to have paid his sons substantial sums of public money with little evidence that they did much work for it. The political parties assured the Committee that they were aware of the problems and would bring about the necessary reforms, but inertia triumphed over initiative and nothing actually happened. It was a fatally missed opportunity.

By the time the greater expenses scandal broke, the Committee was under the chairmanship of Sir Christopher Kelly, a courteous but forceful Whitehall warrior. He was asked to expedite his inquiry and did so, but warned that he would not be rushed into judgement. He won immediate credit for requiring that the political parties' representatives on the Committee should stand aside and take no part in the inquiry. They did not like it but had no alternative. The parties were part of the problem, not the solution.

I met Sir Christopher as the storm was breaking, when the scandal was still in its bath plug phase, and was impressed by his determination and independence of mind. He would be no one's stooge.

'I feel outraged,' he said, 'by some of the things I read in the newspapers, and I think there is more to come out.'

'And what if your Committee's recommendations are rejected?'

'That's an interesting question,' he answered with a twinkle, 'and one that I shall have to ponder at the time.'

Sir Christopher's resignation, however, was unlikely, since the party leaders were committed in advance to accepting almost anything that his Committee proposed. There were some side issues before its members, like the MPs' outside interests, dedicated accommodation for them, and their employment of families. But the central task was relatively straightforward: to turn a system of generous allowances into one of strict and audited expenses.

General Sir Michael Rose, Colonel of the Coldstream Guards, gave evidence to the Committee as a former Adjutant General of the British Army, the Army Board member responsible for pay and allowances. He pointed out that the armed forces had made just such a change 25 years earlier, because *no one should be allowed to benefit financially from an allowance* (his emphasis). 'The system worked well and has lasted to this day.' If the soldiers could do it, then so could the MPs. He concluded: 'As someone who still has residual responsibilities for the welfare and morale of soldiers – many of whom have been appalled by the revelations regarding MPs' expense claims – I would be interested in your comments.'[2]

2. An end to secrecy

We live in a world of instant communications and relative openness, in which the public's right to know is for the first time enshrined in law. The Freedom of Information Act has its necessary exemptions, on grounds including national security, but there is no reason why MPs' addresses should be one of them. Or their expense claims. Or whom they employ on their staff and for how much. Or what they earn for how many hours' work on any other jobs they may have. It is manifestly in the public interest for all of these to be out in the open without exception or redaction.

This requires the repeal of the Julian Lewis motion – in fact there were two of them – on the concealment of MPs' addresses, passed by the House without a vote in July 2008. It would be an admirable gesture if Dr Lewis himself could lead the charge in a spirit of reform and Damascene conversion. He would not do so, of course, because he remained convinced of the rightness of his cause. He told me: 'It is not necessary to put MPs and their families at risk, by publishing their home addresses to the world, in order to prevent some of them from fiddling their expenses. I know that the latter is an important issue, but it is no justification, in the age of the internet and highly organised international terrorism, for putting hundreds of homes and families unnecessarily at risk.'[3]

The House of Commons authorities promise fewer black rectangles in the publication of MPs' expenses in future. But so great is the level of public distrust that any redaction is too much redaction. If we are not allowed to know where MPs live, their flipping of second homes and many of the other abuses will go undetected. The principle would be the same even if our MPs had been shown to be blameless in their expense claims: just as MPs outside London have a right to live to some extent at public expense, so we have a right to know where those second homes are, because we pay for them.

3. Open primaries

In most constituencies for most of the time, the only candidates likely to be elected are those who are nominated by the principal parties themselves – three in England, four in Scotland and Wales. The selection is confined to the membership of a constituency association, sometimes even a sub-committee, choosing from a range of candidates approved by the party centrally: and even then in some circumstances head office has the power to intervene and impose its preferred choice. In elections to the European Parliament, the parties select their candidates in an order decided by them and not by the people: and the order decides who will win and who will lose. It is a process that offers a show of democracy but has about as little to do with government by the people as the old East German *Volkskammer*. It favours the promotion of rubber stamps; and filters out, at an early stage, men and women who would make excellent, thoughtful, independent-minded MPs. It is one of the reasons for the undemocratic mess in which we find ourselves.

The problem is not new, but it is growing more acute. Towards the end of my time in Parliament I served on a Commission on Candidate Selection set up by the Electoral Reform Society. It worked hard, but in my view got nowhere, because the parties were unwilling to give ground to each other or to the voters at large. Its final report was written by the chairman, Peter Riddell of *The Times*, because its party members typically could not agree among themselves on what should be done to open up the process. He described the House of Commons as 'a narrow group of representatives selected by a tiny proportion of the population belonging to parties, for which ever fewer members of the public vote and for whom even fewer people have any feelings of attachment'. In vain did he warn that reform was in the parties' own interest: 'The ultimate verdict lies with the voters since, if the parties do not select the type of candidates that the public wants, they will wither on the vine.'[4]

The open primary breaks the stranglehold on candidate selection. The parties retain a reasonable measure of control. They draw up a shortlist of qualified candidates approved by the party both locally and nationally, but the choice of the candidate to appear on the ballot paper is then made by a postal vote available to everyone on the electoral roll – not just the members of the party's constituency association, but voters of all parties and indeed no party. This has the obvious advantage that the winning candidate is already in some sense the people's choice before the first vote is cast in a general election. It will be objected: would not a party's political opponents vote mischievously for the weakest candidate? Possibly, but in the real world they are seldom that well organised or motivated, and the supposedly weakest candidate anyway may have the broadest appeal. And would not the best-funded candidate have the edge on the others? Possibly again, but the internet and free media are available to all; and the local press will show more interest in an open primary than in a closed-door coronation. Besides, the open primary has already arrived. The Conservatives used it successfully in 2007 in the selection of Boris Johnson as their mayoral candidate in London. And their constituency association in Totnes used it again to choose a successor to the unfortunate Anthony Steen. The only real objection was cost: printing and postal charges made it a £38,000 experiment in open democracy.

The experiment succeeded. Sixteen thousand people took the trouble to vote on a wet weekend in August, clearly not all of them Conservatives. The turnout of almost 25 per cent, not even yet to elect an MP, was quite remarkable. They were asked to choose between three candidates, two with experience as Tory activists and one without much of a political track record at all. They chose the outsider, local GP Dr Sarah Wollaston, who had specifically rejected negative campaigning and represented the clearest break with politics as usual. She did not belong to the political class and expressed no interest in attacking other parties. It was a democratic pick-me-up. It turned the negative story of Anthony Steen's lifestyle into the positive story of a new kind of politics. One of the defeated candidates, Nick Bye, observed: 'Certainly the yah-boo politics that flourishes in the chamber of the House of Commons and in council chambers across the country is unappealing and won't work for any aspiring MP in the primary system.'[5]

The Totnes primary did the Tories so much good, and was so ominous for Labour and the Liberal Democrats, that it left me wondering: where were the so-called progressives in all this? Are they not reformers too? How much longer will they leave their candidate selection to the cliques and cabals of a handful of party activists, half of whom are frequently at daggers drawn with the other half? The scandals have the potential of turning our politics upside down.

There are not many groups of party loyalists who earn a place in constitutional history, but the Totnes Conservative Association may have done just that, with a little help and encouragement from Central Office. In their influential book *The Plan*, two against-the-grain Conservatives, Douglas Carswell MP and Daniel Hannan MEP, make a strong case for the Totnes solution: 'Think, for a moment, of how open primaries would concentrate the minds of British MPs in safe seats. No one, of course, can tell a political party how to select its candidates. But the likelihood is that if one of the political parties adopted open primaries, the others would be obliged to follow.'[6] So farewell to the smoke-filled room: the open primary has arrived and threatens the safest of seats. It is an idea whose time has come. 'This might well be the future', said the Conservative Party chairman Eric Pickles, who hailed the venture as 'a great success for democracy'. It promises to be not a breath but a gale of fresh air.

4. The Alternative Vote

The present voting system of first past the post (FPTP) is tolerably democratic when two parties are dominant and alternate in government: usually, but not always, the party with the most votes wins the most seats. In the multi-party politics which we now have, it distorts the results of a General Election to a point where they never reflect the will of the people. A party can win a substantial majority, as Labour did in 2005, on the votes of less than a quarter of the total electorate. This leaves the great majority of people with no sense of influence over or ownership of their government. It is something done to them, not by them. No wonder that they feel alienated. New Labour was elected in 1997 on a half-promise of electoral reform. The Jenkins Commission, which it set up, proposed a form of proportional representation which was then kicked into the long grass for ten years. Politicians out of power tend to favour electoral reform until they get into power, at which point it seems less attractive to them. The Conservatives, exceptionally, stay bone-headedly loyal to first past the post in good times and bad, even where, as in Scotland, they are permanently disadvantaged by it. They and other opponents of electoral reform argue that FPTP enables governments to govern: it gives them solid majorities. The same can be said of dictatorships with puppet parliaments. And as the power of the Executive has grown, even weak British governments have come to seem more like elective dictatorships. A real democracy requires a better system.

There is a simple and effective one, available at the touch of a referendum. It is called the Alternative Vote (AV). Voters mark their ballot papers not with a cross but with a number, placing the candidates in their order of preference. The candidate with the least support has his or her votes redistributed according to the second preferences. The process continues until one candidate has more than 50 per cent of the votes and is elected. (The AV+ preferred by Lord Jenkins is more complicated and more skewed towards party politics.)

Plain and simple AV, without top-up seats or party lists, is the system used by the Irish to elect their President, and the election in 1990 was an excellent example of its fairness. All three main parties fielded candidates. Fianna Fail's Brian Lenihan received 44 per cent of first-preference votes, Labour's Mary Robinson received 39 per cent, and Fine Gael's Austin Currie 17 per cent. On first past the post Mr Lenihan, a former minister, would have won outright with a minority of the votes. But 80 per cent of Austin Currie's second-preference votes went to Mary Robinson. When these had been redistributed she quite comfortably defeated Mr Lenihan, who was the only Fianna Fail candidate ever to lose an Irish presidential election. She went on to serve as President of Ireland with distinction and the unquestionable support of the majority of the people.

The Alternative Vote has the further advantage that, unlike some other systems, it preserves the link between the MP and the constituency. It also ensures that the winning candidate will be the one most widely supported – or even, in an age of anti-politics, the one least unacceptable – to the most people. The present system does not do that. The winner takes all but the voter loses. Most MPs are elected with less than 50 per cent of the vote. In 1997 the Liberal Democrat Michael Moore became MP for the Scottish constituency of Tweeddale Ettrick and Lauderdale, a four-way marginal, with just 31.2 per cent. It is in the MPs' own interest to have a wider mandate.

The straightforward Alternative Vote offers the parties no complicated top-up options like the system used to elect the Scottish Parliament. Where they win they win and where they lose they lose – but they will win or lose, fair and square, by a more decisive margin. They will object that AV disadvantages them and favours Independents, mavericks, oddballs, football mascots and the like, who are more likely to be the voters' second or third choices. That is one of its blessings. It reflects the will of the people. And, if we are serious about democracy, the mavericks and oddballs who appear on the platform at every by-election should have as fair a chance of election as everyone else. And if elected we can have a reasonable hope that the Independents will not behave like hamsters on a treadmill. The major parties' monopoly of power has been of benefit chiefly to themselves.

5. Unclenching the fist
This is about the culture of Parliament and the role of the parties and especially their enforcers, the whips. The parties are but the shells and husks of the great mass

movements that they used to be, yet they still maintain an arthritic grip on the windpipe of democracy. The whips are the school bullies. They maintain discipline by the threat of punishment or the promise of promotion. It is they and not the MPs at large who decide the membership of the powerful Select Committees. It is they who punish dissent and even abstention. It is they who assign the office space at Westminster, which is not an insignificant form of patronage. Independents and party rebels are disadvantaged. The sheep who let this happen are, in my view, as much to blame as the sheepdogs who make it happen. As with the expenses scandal, this is something that the MPs did to themselves. I was even moved to write a little verse about it:

No need to whip the poor back-bencher
With threats of punishment or censure;
For, seeing what the man will do
Un-whipped, there is no reason to.[7]

Dissatisfaction with the structures of party politics is not confined to the awkward squad: it is felt within the regular parties themselves. In his John Smith Memorial Lecture in July 2009, David Miliband spoke of the need to turn Labour into a different kind of party, 'because the traditional political structures of mainstream political parties are dying. Shrinking membership, declining affinity, fuzzy identity lead many to proclaim that death has already happened, with few tears at the funeral.'[8] An MP wrote to me: 'Disillusioned with SW1 as a new MP,

I began to ask why our party-dominated politics is failing.' MPs are like the tenants of a block of flats which is on the verge of collapse but whose owners insist that all it needs to renew it is a lick of paint.

An act of redemption that could be attempted from the inside is a definitive end to Punch and Judy politics, especially at Prime Minister's Questions. David Cameron promised this once, then admitted going back on his promise, because he was actually rather good at Punch and Judy and his Honourable Friends enjoyed the weekly performances. It is time that he tried again. Apart from the chicanery of the MPs' expenses, there is nothing that so alienates us from our elected representatives as the shouting and jeering, the waving of order papers, the orchestrated cheer-leading, stage-managed antics and mock hostilities of the political class on the floor of the House, like Chesterton's 'huckster who, mocking holy anger, painfully paints his face with rage'. It is about as enlightening as all-in wrestling. David Cameron does not need this. Nor does anyone else. It suggests that the entire political class inhabits another planet. My view of it is uncomplicated: if MPs wish to be more highly regarded, they could always try behaving better. It could and would work wonders for them.

6. A clean sweep of the House

Over many years we have been badly let down by our MPs individually, although not by all of them, by our parties collectively and by the leadership of the House of Commons itself. The weather was made by a government for whom more than three-quarters of the people did not vote and, in recent years, by a non-elected Prime Minister. We were not so much practising democracy as enabling a takeover by the political class. So, after the storm, the remaking of the landscape is now in the voters' hands.

New rules are in place. We have to hope that the new regulatory authority – even with its powers limited more than they should be – will do its best to enforce them. A new Parliament will be elected which, in honesty and competence, must be as unlike the old one as possible. How do we achieve this? Most of all, I think, by paying more attention to the candidate and less to the label. Different voters will apply different tests. These are the ones that work for me.

First, incumbent MPs will be running on their records, which will include not only their votes but their hanging baskets, plasma screens and fitted furniture. Those who have abused the system and not repaid the money and apologised should be defeated by the most electable and honest challenger of any party, or no party. In some cases this may be an Independent, standing possibly for a single term on an anti-miscreant platform. The Independents should be judged as individuals – there is no other way to judge them; but so should the candidates of political parties, who in most constituencies will have the best opportunities to unseat tainted incumbents. There are some MPs who have repaid certain amounts and apologised but still deserve to be retired from Parliament. This is the importance of the wisdom of crowds. Their votes must be concentrated against such people regardless of party. It is the cause, and not the colour of the flag, that matters. There are few safe seats in the old sense any more.

Second, all those who blamed the system, rather than taking personal responsibility, have singled themselves out for the people's de-selection. This includes without exception those whose defence was that they acted within the rules. In Cromwell's words, they have 'grown entirely odious to the whole nation'. A Parliament that lost MPs of the quality of Andrew MacKinlay but kept even one of the expenses swindlers in place would seem to many to be running a deficit on its current account.

Third, for my own part – and others will have other causes and feel as strongly about them – I apply two standards. At the lesser and even ridiculous end of the scale, I could not bring myself to vote for MPs who expect the taxpayers to take care of their grocery bills or supply them with petty cash. At the other and more serious end, I could not put a cross – or in a better electoral system, a number – against the name of an MP who supported the Great Mistake, the war in Iraq, and then continued to justify it, even as a decision taken in good faith. It is all a long time ago now. But they should have known better. And if an MP made a misjudgement on that scale in 2003, might not he or she do the same thing again on any issue and at any time? Such people are dangerous both abroad and at home. They should be found a padded cell or place of safety, other than the House of Lords, where they can do no more harm. Their seats should be taken by new MPs, probably younger but certainly wiser, and with less of a sense of the divine right of Parliament to screw things up.

And finally

As a grace note and act of contrition, the Speaker, the House of Commons Commission and the entire House should make a formal apology to Elizabeth Filkin, the most devoted Commissioner for Standards they ever had, for the unworthy way in which they treated her between 1998 and 2002.

Chapter 16

Days of Reckoning

Straws blew in the wind. The Parliamentary Commissioner for Standards investigated the costs of an MP's sewerage system. Another MP, a burly fellow who was once one of his party's whips, charged the taxpayer £4.95 for the dry-cleaning of a blouse. A third, renowned for his brilliance, claimed £30 for changing two light bulbs. Speaker John Bercow observed that the House of Commons had suffered more damage from the expenses scandal than from anything since the wartime blitz.[1] John Gummer, the mole trap man (Conservative, Suffolk Coastal), was one of many veterans who decided to stand down. Another was Sir Patrick Cormack (Conservative, South Staffordshire) who had twice been a candidate for the Speakership; he referred to 'the unhappy events of recent months' and concluded: 'it is increasingly clear that the new House of Commons will be very different from the old one.'[2] That was not necessarily a cause for regret, for the old House of Commons was so discredited that the new one would have to be different to be respected.

The reforms set out by the Kelly Committee on MPs' expenses were tough, fair, workable and long overdue. MPs outside London could receive taxpayers' money to rent homes but not to buy them. MPs who lived within reach of Westminster would, like their constituents, have to commute to work. The representatives would actually be representative. Their generous resettlement grants on leaving Parliament would be cut back or ended completely. Their high-flying careers would no longer be cushioned by soft landings. Nor, after a five-year phasing out period, would they be allowed to employ their relatives. Husbands and wives might work together in other walks of life, but not in the House of Commons and at the taxpayers' expense. The Fawlty Towers arrangements would have to go.

Backbenchers grumbled, but the party leaders accepted Kelly's proposals in advance. They had to, as a means of undoing the damage done by the years of flipping and swindling and the use of public office for private gain. It would be a steep climb back from the moat and the mole traps to the moral high ground. Professor Sir Ian Kennedy, the first chairman of the new Independent Parliamentary Standards Authority, said: 'It will take time and effort to earn back the trust that has been lost.' He promised that his IPSA would be truly independent. Yet its powers were limited. Just as its members had been appointed by the House of Commons, they could also be dismissed by the House of Commons. Most of the praetorian guard who had led the resistance to the publication of MPs' expenses were still in place. They could be relied on for a last-ditch defence of the privileges so dear to them. You could almost hear the sound of their trenching tools around the Palace of Westminster. Their commitment to reform had all the tensile strength of a bowl of porridge.

Sir Ian Kennedy could have opened his innings by endorsing in full the Kelly Committee recommendations. He pointedly refrained from doing so. 'Both Sir Christopher and Sir Ian,' said a joint statement, 'are clear about the task ahead and the direction of travel.' The weasel words were strung together like imitation pearls. There were fears of backroom deals in the House of Commons, which is the cooking pot of compromises and the stately home of stitch-ups. A group of 37 MPs, including Keith Vaz, signed a motion urging Sir Ian to be reasonable and proportionate and not to penalise those who had made questionable claims in the past. Silk cushions, anyone? Hanging baskets? Mystery mortgages? Never mind the direction of travel: somewhere down the track Sir Ian could, if he wished, unhitch his IPSA from Sir Christopher's locomotive, shunt it into a siding and leave it to let the long grass grow over it.

The government had the opportunity, in the Queen's Speech announcing its legislative programme, to signal its intention of turning the Kelly Committee's proposals into law. They received no mention at all. Either the issue mattered or it did not. It clearly did not. The entire upheaval might as well not have happened for all that the speech took account of it. Sir Christopher gently expressed his disappointment.

At this point the long grass threatened to grow over everything. At the request of the House of Commons Sir Thomas Legg, a former civil servant and Whitehall luminary, had been reviewing the MPs' expenses one by one, and telling them how much they should repay. (There were no known cases of under-claiming; see Epilogue.) Again the party leaders ordered compliance; and again the back-sliders back-slid. The Members Estimate Committee, leading its usual fighting retreat on their behalf, ruled that they should have a right of appeal; 80 diehards who felt themselves to be victims went down that route. Sir Paul Kennedy, a former judge, was appointed to adjudicate their appeals. So along with Sir Ian, Sir Christopher and Sir Thomas, a courtly quartet was now completed with the arrival of Sir Paul: the clean-up process had as many knights in play as a game of chess. Miscreant MPs seeking re-election were given a chance, for a time at least, to argue that the cases against them were still under review and that they would, in the end, be vindicated. For connoisseurs of prevarication, that had been Neil Hamilton's defence in 1997, and it had been strong enough to ensure his re-selection.

The MPs serving on the Standards and Privileges Committee, supposedly the custodians of the reputation of the House, proved themselves once more to be unequal to the task of self-regulation. A number of them had problems with their own expenses, including their newly appointed chairman, David Curry, who resigned.

In their reports on the scandal-driven cases that came before them – flipping, swindling and all the rest of it – they rallied to the defence of their kind. Tony McNulty (Labour, Harrow East) was made to apologise for allowing his parents' home in the constituency to masquerade as his own, but to pay back only £13,837 of the £72,500 in taxpayers' money that this arrangement had earned him over a six-year period. The *Daily Telegraph* observed that the committee's decision 'exemplifies everything that was rotten with the now discredited system of MPs' allowances'.[3] Nothing forgotten and nothing learned: the parliamentary Bourbons strolled on, and the plundering of the public purse continued.

A fresh encyclopaedia of MPs' expenses was published in December 2009, less redacted than the first but in most cases just as extraordinary, and with many of the same MPs leading the cast of characters. Twenty-one had flipped their second homes in a year. The claims for reimbursement ranged from the trivial to the monumental. At one end of the scale were 30p for an Ikea carrier bag (Siôn Simon, Labour, Birmingham Erdington) and £36.66 for a set of three garlic slicers (James Arbuthnot, Conservative, Hampshire North East), and at the other more than £20,000 for the repair of the roof and bell tower of Frampton Hall, the stately home of Quentin Davies (Conservative turned Labour) in Lincolnshire. 'The bell tower is an integral part of the roof,' he told the Fees Office, 'if it had not been repaired it would have smashed through the roof.' He later maintained that he had not intended to claim for the bell tower; but it remained on the record, along with the duck island and the moat, as one of the enduring symbols of the scandal, an epitome of entitlement and an icon of impenitence. So great was the public outcry that, reluctantly and late in the day, the government changed its mind and agreed that the standards authority should have limited powers of enforcement.

Jacqui Smith, the former Home Secretary of bath plug fame, made further claims of £611 for a double bed from John Lewis and £555.74 for a TV set, her third in four years, for her house in Redditch. When the earlier complaint against her came before the Standards and Privileges Committee, she was required to apologise for designating her first home as her second home, but had to pay back none of the £100,000 from which she had benefited as a result of not knowing where she lived. Yet she showed in the end unusual contrition in admitting that her expenses had been to some extent a disgrace, and implicitly ruling herself out of a peerage, in that 'disgraced MPs should not go to the House of Lords'.[4]

The ousted MPs, when they spoke at all, were publicly contrite but privately indignant. The Tory backwoodsmen, very few of whom had flipped their homes, were on their way to enforced retirement while other MPs more useful to the leadership, including a number of conspicuous swindlers, remained on the front bench. One of the aggrieved old-timers wrote to me: 'Those MPs who were transparent, i.e. produced receipts for their allowance claims, are the ones who have been most vilified … The vortex in which I was plunged was quite horrific.'

Among the Independents seeking advice was an aspiring candidate summoning up the courage and support to take on one of the most notorious crooks in the House. The MP's personal claims had been outrageous, but he was so senior and influential that his party would not disown him. Over many years he had traded in favours and bound his constituents to him by a spider's web of obligations, real or perceived, so that at election time his machine did not so much deliver the votes as harvest them. A climate of fear prevailed in his constituency. Many of his former supporters wished to see the back of him, but feared for the impact on themselves and their families if they said so publicly. One was a businessman of Asian origin whose family had left the sub-continent, in a previous generation, in part because of the graft and corruption rife in Indian provincial government. And now it was taking root in a British city.

It was remarkable, but not surprising, how few of the mainstream miscreants were forced to quit by their parties. Backbenchers were vulnerable to de-selection, but front-benchers were not. However, if the parties would not dislodge them perhaps the people could. And so there began, quietly and across the country, a number of ad hoc meetings to identify electable Independents to challenge those MPs who hung on against the tide of the times in their constituency fortresses.

One of these was Hazel Blears, MP for Salford. In September 2009, at a 'Hazel Must Go' rally in her constituency, I was struck by the strength and depth of the feeling against her. But I thought it peculiar, and perhaps imprudent, that the campaign to unseat her adopted a manifesto – and a hard left one at that – before it had even selected a candidate.

The defenders of status quo politics – at the most, there were no more than half a dozen of these impenitents – complained that our ancient liberties would be threatened by an avalanche of so-called 'celebrity candidates'. They need not have worried. As it turned out it was a small but forceful avalanche of just one, Esther Rantzen in Luton South. She might have been joined by Terry Waite in Bury St Edmunds, where he lived, but he was so committed to other causes that, surely to the relief of the incumbent, he concluded that a challenge to David Ruffley MP (£2,175 for a Harrods widescreen television) was unlikely to be one of them. But he urged other Independents to stand with his support, not subservient to party dogma, and bring about the necessary reforms: 'This is a unique point in the history of our country. The call goes out to the country to find other people who are willing to stand for no other reason than that they desire to see the United Kingdom develop a fair and just society where tradition is respected and Parliament is truly a parliament of the people. Let us hope that such people will come forward in the coming months – and, if you are such, more power to your elbow!'[5]

The weather of politics was also changing, in immeasurable but very real ways. Alongside the second tranche of expenses abuses, the Chilcot Inquiry opened into an earlier scandal, the decision to invade Iraq on the basis of false information. Former ambassadors, generals and senior advisers to the then Prime Minister, Tony Blair, were more forthcoming than they had been earlier about this failure, not only of intelligence in both its senses, but of parliamentary democracy itself. The former Director of Public Prosecutions, Sir Ken Macdonald, called it '[a] foreign policy disgrace of epic proportions'. In a widely quoted analysis he wrote: 'The tax on dishonesty is rising. Now our system has to prove itself again and again ... Naturally, this is a less comfortable world for people in power, but it is a much better world for everyone else.'[6]

A second front was opening in the House of Lords. 103 peers had claimed more than £50,000 in expenses, tax-free and at taxpayers' expense, in a single year. Under the pressure of the Commons scandal, the more reasonable peers – who were actually a majority – did their best to put their House in order. They agreed to a review of their expenses by the Senior Salaries Review Board. It recommended a cut of £34 in their overnight allowance, and a maximum of £200 for turning up at all. Others of the ermine-clad were not impressed. One peer called the payment 'derisory' and 'an insult'. A cross-bench hereditary, Lord Palmer, was one of those ill at ease with the proposed economies, including an end to automatic first-class travel for peers and their spouses: 'The idea of having to share a [sleeping] compartment with a complete stranger or indeed another noble lord is completely unthinkable.' Baroness Shepherd, a minister in John Major's government, added: 'Your spouse is going to be in the guard's van.'[7]

At about this time I was chatting to a policeman I knew outside the House of Lords. A couple of young Australians came up and, seeing the grandeur of the place, asked: 'Excuse me, but is this a church?' 'No,' I said, 'it's a den of thieves – and there's an even bigger one next door.' The judgement was actually not mine but that of a friend, a truly Honourable Member who, having done his time in one House was elevated to the other. He was appalled by what he found there and some of the company he was keeping, noble lords (a few of them former cabinet ministers) who were milking the system to the limit, turning up for just a few minutes a day and claiming generous allowances for next to nothing – nice work if they could get it, which they did. 'You've got to sort this place out,' said my friend. But I had to face the fact that the reputation of the Commons had sunk even lower than when I entered it.

The Commons was where the focus rightly remained. As the election approached, the danger was not that the voters would forget their MPs' misdemeanours. The danger was that they would remember them only too well and show their disaffection by supporting extremists or by turning their backs on the whole charade and staying away from the polls. The 'stay-at-home' and 'none-of-the-above' vote would certainly be substantial but its effect would be, perversely, to cancel the long-awaited judgement day, reprieve the villains by default and entrench the political class still further in its positions of power and privilege. I did what I could for Independents – not all, but those who seemed the most electable – working quietly behind the scenes and speaking and campaigning for them wherever possible. The failure of our politics was all but impossible to put into words, although of course I had a go at it.

> *In discharge of their parliamentary duties –*
> *And, incidentally, the pursuit of power –*
> *Our MPs perpetrated some real beauties,*
> *The hanging baskets, duck house and bell tower.*
> *Wodehouse, you should be living at this hour:*
> *Did Blandings Castle also have a moat?*
> *Forgive the idiom, but what a shower!*
> *And all elected on the people's vote.*
> *They may have done some service now and then,*
> *But took us for a ride and robbed us rotten.*
> *Surely we shall not be deceived again,*
> *Nor will their misdemeanours be forgotten.*
> *Henceforth let no one ever have the nerve,*
> *To say we get the Members we deserve.*

Chapter 17

Restoring Trust

Exceptional times call for exceptional measures to be taken by our political leaders with the earned trust of the people.

I believe that internationally we are living in the most dangerous times since 1945. I don't get this from the press, which has significantly retreated from the real world into one whose values are those of the *Big Brother* house, but from my own experiences in Iraq, Afghanistan, Somalia, Darfur, the Democratic Republic of Congo and elsewhere. Our children and grand-children face challenges which we did not. Great tides of refugees in their tens and hundreds of thousands are flooding across borders within Africa, and out of Africa into Yemen, southern Europe and the Canary Islands. Nuclear weapons and failed states are prolifer-ating. Piracy threatens the sea lanes. Natural disasters are increasing in number and intensity. New wars are being fought in new ways. Some of them are wars for natural resources, chiefly oil and water: the conflict in

Darfur may be, among other things, the first war of climate change. Others are the Caliphate wars of militant Islam, open-ended and transnational. Nothing in our history ever prepared us, even in our other three Afghan wars, for the phenomenon of the child suicide bomber. The death toll rises. Our present Afghan war, like its three predecessors, is probably unwinnable. Expect no tank battles: today's wars are fought among the people and for their allegiance. The use of force alone will not prevail.

For much of our history, we British have felt threatened by strong states – Spain, France, Germany and the Soviet Union – and prepared our defences accordingly. Now we are threatened by weak ones, of which Afghanistan and Somalia are the outstanding examples. The intelligence services and Chiefs of Staff know that. The Islamic warriors have opened a new front.

Conditions at home are hardly more settled and certain. We are plunged into the deepest recession in living memory. We shall not escape from it by quantitative easing, by double-counting our dwindling assets or by pawning our grandchildren's futures. We have lost faith in our bankers almost as much as in our politicians. Both have been seen to bail themselves out at our expense: and both will enjoy the most generous pensions with which to gild their retirements. We have been paying our taxes for fraudsters, as well as honest retirees, to live in comfort for the rest of their days.

The generations are also disconnected. The older one worries about material conditions, declining investments, quantitative easing and all the rest of the fallout from the recession. The younger one is concerned about global warming and its future, if it has one, on an inhabitable planet. The art of political communication fails us even, and perhaps especially, in an age of spin. We need a George Orwell and don't have one.

Such is our predicament. It cannot be addressed by politicians who have lost our trust because they have picked our pockets. Some of their peculations may seem trivial: a swimming pool boiler, a barbecue, a garden shed, a gazebo, a dozen wine glasses, a patio heater, a mole trap, a love seat – all claimed at public expense and, all added up together, costing much less than the bailout of a bank. Some of their more modest claims may actually have been justified; it does cost money to fix the central heating or repair the roof of a second home. But the small scale swiftly shades into the large scale. As the late Senator Everett Dirksen of Illinois famously observed: 'A billion here, a billion there, and pretty soon you are talking about real money.' And it is the perception – no, not just the perception but the reality – that the system is corrupt, or open to corruption, and that so many of the MPs working within it have been corrupt – not just a few, but maybe even a majority – that has shattered public confidence. Half of the Parliamentary Conservative Party either volunteered or were required to pay back money that they should not have claimed in the first place, to a total of at least £125,000 (plus what they had already returned to the Fees Office). All three leaders of the main parties were among the refunders.

We used to believe, in more settled times, that while many MPs may be hard to admire, our own was hard-working and honest. And some still are. But the abuse has been sustained and systematic. And our own MP, as likely as not, has been part of it.

The expenses scandal had the force of a tidal wave. The closest analogy I could think of was the fishing harbour in the town of Galle in southern Sri Lanka on Boxing Day 2004. When the tsunami struck, it had the effect of sucking the water out of the harbour before it came surging back. For a while, fishing boats were left lying stricken on their sides, old wrecks and submerged obstructions were revealed, and ugly, repellent creatures, previously underwater, were seen slithering and wriggling in the mud. So it was with the House of Commons: the tide went out and the low life was exposed. We had long suspected it was there, but had no idea of the scale of it.

Another analogy came to mind, from my time as MP for Tatton. At the Northwich end of the constituency, some of the open spaces included contaminated land from the days when the town was a major centre of the chemical industry. ICI had closed its plants and moved elsewhere; and the old sites had been systematically cleaned up to be turned into parks and playgrounds. The House of Commons too was contaminated land. Some of the corruption was out in the open, but it was a reasonable guess that there was a great deal still remaining to be unearthed. A surface clean-up would not do the job.

A third analogy – and then I am done with analogies. It comes, like the tsunami, from my work for UNICEF. When a natural disaster strikes anywhere in the world, the aid agencies and national governments have learned from experience not just to rebuild things as they were. Things as they were, vulnerable structures put up in the wrong places, were actually part of the problem. The new theory goes beyond restoring the status quo. It is called Building Back Better.

Building Back Better is now our political challenge. The expenses tsunami was not a natural but a man-made disaster. It did not have to happen. It was a conspicuous act of parliamentary self-harm. The opportunity that this leaves us is once-in-a-lifetime. If it had been less calamitous – perhaps, if the redactions had succeeded in blurring the reality – we would not have this chance. But we do have it. We are in this together, responding as a people against the corruption of a failed political class. We have a chance to revive our democracy, to erect new structures in place of the old, and to populate them with MPs who are in politics for what they can put into it rather than for what they can get out of it. There are such MPs even now in the House of Commons. The truly Honourable Members belong to all parties. They are like a tattered, ragged regiment which has been on the defensive for far too long, is low on morale and ammunition, and needs reinforcements to hold the line before advancing. If our democracy still has life in it, those reinforcements will arrive after the next election with the massive intake of new MPs, who will have learned from the past without being tainted by it. This will be the river flowing through Parliament to cleanse it. (I said I had done with analogies, but I obviously hadn't – a promise no sooner made than broken!)

We have been there before and will doubtless go there again. The reform of our democracy is constant work in progress. The tide of public trust lies at its lowest ebb in my lifetime. Our MPs' actions speak louder than their words. Those who wax lyrical about the Mother of Parliaments have often proved to be among its greatest scoundrels, and those who have accused it of corruption among its greatest champions. Eight years before he was finally elected as MP for Oldham in 1832 – an election made possible by the passage of the Great Reform Act – William Cobbett wrote in his *Grammar of the English Language*: 'Nouns of number, or Multitude, such as Mob, Parliament, Rabble, House of Commons, Regiment, Court of King's Bench, Den of Thieves and the like.'[1] He continued to attack it for all the time he was in it. His nearest equivalent today is Dennis Skinner, Labour MP for Bolsover, a constant scourge and devoted parliamentarian.

A lesser scandal would not have provoked such a clamour for reform. Adversity can actually be quite useful. I experienced this in my war-zone years when, rather unexpectedly, I was once bombed by the Serbs and robbed by the French on the same day. (The Serbs fired the mortar and the French ran the UN's field hospital.) Although I took a dim view of it at the time, it taught me what not to take for granted, and to look at the world in an entirely different way: from that point on, I saw every day as the first day of the rest of my life. I still do.

Now we know what we know about our MPs' behaviour, our politics too will not be the same again. A presumption of honesty will not be theirs to enjoy or ours to take for granted. Some may believe that the expenses scandal was just a passing storm, that other news stories have taken its place – swine flu, the death of a pop star, the bugging of celebrities' phones, and so on; and that the House of Commons can return, with a little cosmetic surgery, to what it was before. I think that this is unlikely for a number of reasons. The first is that the shock felt by the MPs themselves has been so intense, that out of sheer self-respect they will never again allow themselves to be in a position to be so comprehensively reviled. The second is that with the massive influx of new Members in the next Parliament, it will have a different look about it. The third is that the rules on expenses and allowances will be clearly set out. And the fourth is that, if the Independent Parliamentary Standards Authority is to mean anything, the rules will be rigorously enforced and offenders made to pay the penalty, from fines and suspension all the way to expulsion from the House. Somewhere within the fine print of the new legislation there has to lie a shadow of the gallows.

The usual suspects made the usual excuses. It was time to draw a line under the scandal and move on – or, in the words of the veteran MP and Deputy Speaker Sir Michael Lord, 'To put it to bed'. Oh no it wasn't. It was time to examine it, analyse it and prod it into revealing its secrets. For what is the point of enduring this dishevelment if we are not prepared to learn from it? There is ample evidence that we are learning from it. Candidates are falling over each other with promises to be frugal, to post all their expenses on the internet, even to pay for their own gardening and to travel by train in standard class. This is political climate change.

Parties, like species, adapt to a changing environment or they die. The Conservatives were so deeply involved in the expenses scandal, on the front bench as well as the back, that it took some agility, and nerve, for them to reinvent themselves as the anti-politics party, turning their back on their past. Yet that is to some extent what they achieved with their new-look candidate in Norwich North and their successful open primary in Totnes. I have been arguing for years, from a non-party standpoint, for a politics that is more of a dialogue and less of a dogfight: for something less confrontational, kinder, gentler and closer to the people. Now the Conservatives are promising it – or at least some of them are. I do not expect their old guard to fall into line, but they have a party chairman who understands. 'When we go in hard,' says Eric Pickles MP, 'we fail.' Nick Bye, one of the defeated candidates in their Totnes primary, wrote of his hustings experience: 'I made the mistake of using one of my favourite lines of attack. "One of the great myths of politics is that the Liberal Democrats are such nice people" went down a storm in front of the party executive. But in front of the wider audience it fell as flat as a pancake.'[2] The old applause lines no longer work. When politicians generally have fallen into disrepute, their attacks on each other will be counter-productive. This too is political climate change.

When a party is challenged from the right, it will move to the right to assimilate the challenge. When it is challenged from the left, it will move to the left. But when something unprecedented occurs, as happened with the sudden disgrace of so many Honourable Members, and it is challenged from the centre ground by ordinary, usually non-party voters concerned about its behaviour – whether in its manner of campaigning or in the integrity or otherwise of its MPs – then it will respond to that challenge too. So will the other parties and candidates. They will seek to outdo each other in being more frugal, more transparent and, yes, even more humble than they were in the halcyon years before the scandal. Our politicians, not previously known for their humility, have been chastened by the force of public anger. They have received one hell of a blow to their self-esteem, and will not carry on as before, unless the political wilderness appeals to them. A party that carries on as if nothing has altered risks extinction as well as defeat. This also is political climate change. And it is part of a very British revolution.

It was one of the refrains of the save-our-MPs brigade that, despite a few problems here and there, we could pride ourselves on standards in public life that were the envy of our neighbours in Europe and of the world. It was a hard case to make in the summer of 2009, when our politicians had turned themselves into the laughing stock of the continent. The Italian newspaper *Corriere Della Sera* wrote: 'The government is sinking fast, the electorate is demotivated, tired and angry.' But the Justice Secretary, Jack Straw, bravely had a go at it in front of the Kelly Committee: 'It happens that our politics in this country compared to many, many countries is clean and transparent. Some of our continental colleagues are astonished that we should be getting ourselves into this kind of a paddy over a few thousand pounds. ... My Italian colleagues are incredulous that we should have got ourselves into this situation.'[3]

Sir Christopher Kelly was unimpressed: 'It was a convenient assumption I think – a comfortable assumption that we all shared – that politics in this country were cleaner than most other places. I think that is not universally true.'

The way that Italians practise their democracy, and the extraordinary tolerance they extend to their President, on issues involving more than a few thousand pounds, and on whom he promotes for the most personal reasons, are matters entirely for them. But we do not need to take Italian lessons in how to practise ours.

Ours is peculiar to us. Ever since the Civil War – perhaps because of the Civil War – we have a record of continuous and inherited government unmatched elsewhere in the world. We have preferred evolution to revolution. No assembly of MPs has been thrown out since Cromwell's dismissal of the 'mercenary wretches' of the Rump Parliament in 1653. We have had an attempt to blow the place up, which we celebrate every year with bonfires and fireworks, but nothing since then so seriously root-and-branch. We have had regime change both royal and political, as dynasties and governments have been challenged, displaced and succeeded by each other. We have had occasional uprisings of the people, from the Peterloo massacre to the poll tax riots, usually suppressed by the civil power, and sometimes by the military. We have danced with democracy, two steps forward and one step back, ever since the Great Reform Act. (Lately it has seemed more like one step forward and two steps back.) But we, so martial and imperial abroad – and even now engaged in yet another Afghan war – have proved at home to be a quiet, deferential, shoulder-shrugging people even in the face of the most dreadful abuses of power. We lowered our pikestaffs and went off to the pub. The great upheaval never actually happened. G.K. Chesterton caught this exactly in his poem 'The Secret People', which I quoted extensively in the Tatton campaign of 1997.

> It may be we shall rise the last as Frenchmen rose the
> first,
> Our wrath come after Russia's wrath and our wrath be
> the worst.
> It may be we are meant to mark with our riot and our
> rest
> God's scorn for all men governing. It may be beer is best.
> But we are the people of England; and we have not
> spoken yet.
> Smile at us, pay us, pass us. But do not quite forget.

And that is why the response to the expenses scandal has been, and remains, such a typically British affair. The people have spoken, loud and clear, but have only been half heeded. The revolution has partly succeeded and partly failed. It has gone half circle. It has lasted beyond normal time into extra time and beyond. It has changed the weather and the landscape of politics, yet faltered before the last-ditch resistance of the entrenched political class. It has driven scores of deplorable MPs into well-deserved retirement, but others remain of equal delinquency, even on the front benches, to be dismissed or defeated in the months or years ahead. We shall not allow them to outlast us. We shall have to keep at it – or, as the soldiers say, to crack on – and we should learn from these best of British in Helmand Province: 'The Bugle Major sounded the advance and it would have been heard right across the valley as the sun slipped behind the ridge.' So we also should take courage. There is an enemy closer to home to be defeated. It is work in progress, make-or-break time, now or never, urgently requiring shoulders to the wheel of reform and retribution. And it has taught us two lessons about our MPs that we shall not lightly forget.

The first is that it is not their Parliament: it is our Parliament.

And the second is that politics is too important to be left to the politicians. They are not to be trusted with it.

Epilogue

The clinching report by Sir Thomas Legg on MPs' abuse of their expenses was published on 4 February 2010. Sir Thomas, a former senior civil servant, was unsparing in his judgements. He described the system of allowances as deeply flawed and attacked the culture of deference which had allowed the scandal to take root and to flourish. He convincingly disposed of the myth that only a small minority of MPs had misbehaved – the 'few bad apples' theory so popular with the defenders of the political class. Of the 750 cases that had come before him, of sitting or recently retired Members, he concluded that 392 had claimed and received public money which they should not have done, and which they would now have to pay back. The inference that the voters could draw from this was that *more than half the Honourable Members had acted like crooks.*

The largest refunder was the local government minister Barbara Follett, required to hand back £42,458, most of it spent on her personal security. She apologised and called it a 'sad and sorry episode'. Seven other MPs, all of them Tories, had to return more than £20,000 each.

This was a cross-party scandal and the scale of the over-claiming had not been trivial. The *Daily Telegraph* thundered: 'It was not just that it exposed the dishonesty and greed of many MPs; it has also done untold damage to our democracy, which only the election of a new parliament can repair.'[1]

It will take more than that, since despite the damning evidence against them, some of the rogues were likely to be re-elected. I wrote in *The Times*, on the day after the Legg Report, of an MP widely known to be more than ordinarily corrupt both inside and outside his constituency, but who because of his seniority faced no threat of de-selection by his party. And there were others – too many others – whose electoral survival would prevent a clean break with the past. The parties' disciplinary procedures had been partial and incomplete. They had ejected some of the miscreants and protected others. There would be an overflow of disrepute from one House of Commons to the next.

But some did step down. Every week brought news of an MP with a questionable expenses record deciding to retire from public life. There was always a cover story. The MP had a health problem, or had found fresh challenges elsewhere, or wished to make an impact on global warming or some other good cause, or whatever. But the people knew. The people always know. There was even a certain symmetry to it: the culture of dishonesty was so deeply ingrained that those who had performed scandalously on the public stage could not even make their exits without falsehood. It would be a test of the parties' determination to make a new start that not one of the tainted retirees would be rewarded, as so often in the past, with a seat in the House of Lords. The Lords had troubles enough of its own without inheriting a load of damaged goods from the Commons.

The police had also been active. After a six-month investigation the Crown Prosecution Service announced that it was in the public interest to bring charges under the Theft Act against three MPs: Elliot Morley (Labour, Scunthorpe), David Chaytor (Labour, Bury North) and Jim Devine (Labour, Livingstone). A Conservative peer, Lord Hanningfield, was also charged. The three MPs denied wrong-doing and promised to defend themselves robustly. They were reported to have consulted constitutional lawyers to advise them about precedents going back to the Bill of Rights in 1689. Their defence might lie in the doctrine of parliamentary privilege: because they had been acting in their capacity as MPs, only Parliament could deal with them and they could not properly be brought before a criminal court. If that were to be established it would confirm the popular view that in all this lamentable business there was one law for the Honourable Members and another for everyone else. And a principle established to defend the people against the Crown would be subverted to defend MPs against the people. This also became an election issue. The three MPs were suspended from the Labour Party and their 'golden parachutes' (resettlement grants on leaving the House) were also suspended while the cases against them continued.

The House of Commons was slowly edging towards a more accountable system. Most of Sir Christopher Kelly's proposed reforms were being implemented, if not all. The political class fought on in its last ditch. The Independent Parliamentary Standards Authority, still in its infancy, appeared already to be in some measure a creature of the House of Commons and not as independent as its name implied. Sir Christopher's annual report had an air of exasperation about it, like that of a schoolmaster assessing a recalcitrant pupil. He lamented the failure of leadership in the House and in the political parties in the scandal's early stages: 'One of the sadnesses of the expenses episode is that a significant number of MPs had concerns about the situation. But little was done until a good deal of damage had been done to the reputation of the House.'[2] And before a committee of MPs his patience snapped: 'All of you are guilty of having gone along with a system which you must have known was flawed, even if you were not personally guilty.'[3]

Right to the end the Honourable Members retained a certain vaudeville appeal. Some could have qualified for the OBE – as On Board Entertainers. The democratic tragedy of the expenses scandal had some comic repercussions, especially in my home county of Suffolk. John Gummer, the retiring Conservative MP for Suffolk Coastal, was required by Sir Thomas Legg to pay back £29,398 of the expenses he had received. Some of his better known claims were for the elimination of garden pests. I suggested to Graham Dines, the political editor of the *East Anglian Daily Times*, whom I had known from my time as a Euro candidate, that he should write a piece on the influence of moles in Suffolk's politics. And I went further than that – I even wrote it for him:

> *John Gummer MP's undisputed role*
> *Is that of a Conservative grandee.*
> *He's also known, unreasonably perhaps,*
> *For garden pests, for moles and for mole traps.*
> *So Suffolk people find it rather neat,*
> *And even democratically droll,*
> *That his son Ben is trying to unseat*
> *The MP for Ipswich, who is Mr Mole.*

The issues were more serious than mole-catching. Our system of representative government, which we had supposed to be a model for the world – with so many imitations of the Commons from Canada to Barbados to Malawi – turned out to be its laughing stock. Whoever would have thought that half our MPs would be untrustworthy in the simple management of their accounts? That the accountants themselves would so often have rubber-stamped their raids on public funds? That anyone could have believed that hanging baskets were a parliamentary expense? Or duck islands? Or bell towers? That self-regulation would have failed so dismally? That some of the disgraced Honourable Members, pushing their privileges to the limit, would see themselves as being beyond the reach of the common law? And that the integrity of the voting system itself would be compromised by extensions of the postal ballot that were an open invitation to widespread fraud? Maybe we had more to learn from other democracies than to teach them, certainly from Portugal and South Africa in terms of voter turnout. As for the rest of Africa, in 2005 Robert Mugabe had offered to send a team of Zimbabwean observers to the United Kingdom to ensure a fair result. And why not? Our system was on the sick list. The example that we set to Zimbabwe and elsewhere was hardly that of a functioning, open democracy.

The campaign to elect a new, and perhaps better, House of Commons began in earnest in January 2010. Public trust in public life was a major political issue as it had not been since 1997, yet the contenders did not come to it with clean hands. One of the ironies of the campaign was the spectacle of flippers and swindlers from one party seeking to claim the moral high ground from the flippers and swindlers of another. The Conservative Party chairman, Eric Pickles MP, rightly bemoaned the 'massive democratic deficit ... people are increasingly disillusioned and angry with our political system'.[4]

It is hard to know how historians will judge us, but the great contest of 2010 may come to be known as the pot and kettle election, or perhaps the frying pan and the fire.

A return to parliamentary health could be helped by the election of Independents and independent-minded MPs within the parties. Terry Waite hoped for a block of 25 Independents. Although he is not standing himself because he is over-committed elsewhere, he would have had a good chance against the Conservative David Ruffley in Bury St Edmunds.

While always reluctant to disagree with Terry, I felt that he was being over-optimistic. It was the best of times for Independents because of the expenses scandal and the manifest failures of the party system. But it was also the worst of times, because with an election approaching, the parties were gearing up their juggernauts yet again, often fuelled by cash from questionable sources. The usual pressures on insurgent candidates would be intensified by a new feature of the 2010 campaign, the televised debates from which all but the main parties would be excluded. The little platoons would find it hard going against the big battalions. I felt that we would be doing well to return half a dozen Independents, Richard Taylor in Wyre Forest and Dai Davies in Blaenau Gwent, plus a handful of others. Even that would be an advance on what we had before.

The informal organisation of the Independent Network, which existed to help Independents help each other, would never be a match for the political parties, still less a political party itself, but it provided a degree of co-ordination for insurgent candidates trying to challenge the discredited systems and practices of the past. It also helped answer the question: We know what Independents are *against*, but what are they actually *for*? At Terry Waite's request I drafted a set of principles which the Independent Network circulated. The hoped-for block of Independents would abide by the seven principles of public life; their policies would not be racist or discriminatory; they would be answerable only to their constituents and their consciences; they would be a force for honest politics; their expenses would be modest and transparent; they would have a parliamentary leader but no whip; and they would resist abuses of power by the Executive. Nothing revolutionary there – but a Parliament of Independents would not have fallen into the disrepute of the one that was now in its death throes. Nor would it have voted for a war based on a falsehood.

Oliver Cromwell might have disagreed – there was no Legg Report in 1653 – but the House of Commons of 2005 will go down as the most corrupt and venal in our history – not necessarily for what it was, but for what it was perceived to be. Others may have contained as many rascals, but as a result of the exposure of the expenses claims, the facts and figures for this one were in the public domain: a little over half of all Honourable Members had engaged in dishonourable activities, ranging from petty fiddling to outright fraud: a den of thieves indeed. And here was a lesson for the new intake of MPs whose mission was in part to clear up the mess that they had inherited. They were replacing so many of the old brigade who, for several parliaments, had served their constituents and their parties with apparent distinction, not to say self-satisfaction, and some of whom had knighthoods to go with it, but whose time in the House would be remembered only for their manner of leaving it.

So the Duck Island Parliament passed into history unmourned except by its inmates.

Notes

Chapter 1

1. Evidence to the Kelly Committee, 6 June 2009.
2. BBC interview, 29 June 2009.
3. *The Guardian*, 11 July 2009.
4. *New York Times*, 20 May 2009.
5. *New York Times*, 20 May 2009.

Chapter 2

1. Evidence to the Kelly Committee, 23 June 2009.
2. Evidence to the Kelly Committee, 16 July 2009.
3. *Sunday Times*, 21 May 2006.
4. Speech introducing the annual report of the Committee on Standards, 27 March 2007.
5. *The Guardian*, 29 March 2009.
6. *The Truth That Sticks*, Icon Books, 2008, p. 266.
7. Evidence to the Kelly Committee, 29 June 2009.
8. Evidence to the Kelly Committee, 29 June 2009.
9. Evidence to the Kelly Committee, 30 June 2009.
10. *Hansard*, 20 April 2007.
11. *Daily Telegraph*, 23 May 2009.
12. BBC *Newsnight*, 24 June 2009.
13. *Daily Telegraph*, 24 June 2009.
14. *Daily Telegraph*, 20 June 2000.

Chapter 3

1. Committee on Standards in Public Life, 8th Report, November 2002.
2. *Daily Telegraph*, 16 May 2009.
3. *Wilmslow Express*, 28 May 2009.
4. *The Independent*, 3 June 2009.
5. *East Anglian Daily Times*, 25 June 2009.
6. *The Independent*, 27 June 2009.

Chapter 4

1. *Daily Mail*, 14 August 2009.
2. *Hansard*, 1 July 2009.
3. *Daily Mail*, 25 July 2009.
4. *Daily Telegraph*, 14 May 2009.
5. *Daily Telegraph*, 16 May 2009.

Chapter 5

1. *Hansard*, 17 July 2008.
2. Letter to the author, 13 July 2009.
3. *The Guardian*, 21 June 2009.
4. Committee on Standards in Public Life, 8th report, November 2002.

Chapter 6

1. *The Independent*, 25 July 2009.
2. *Hansard*, 8 July 2009.
3. *Hansard*, 14 July 2009.

Chapter 7

1. *Hansard*, 23 October 2000.
2. *The Observer*, 19 April 2009.
3. *Daily Mail*, 17 May 2009.
4. *Hansard*, 19 May 2009.
5. *Daily Mail*, 23 June 2009.
6. *Hansard*, 22 June 2009.
7. *Hansard*, 22 June 2009.
8. *Sunday Times*, 2 August 2009.

Chapter 8

1. ComRes poll, 23 May 2009.
2. *The Guardian*, Comment is Free, 25 May 2009.
3. *The Prince*, Penguin Classics, London, 2009, p. 90.
4. *The Guardian*, 29 July 2009.
5. *The Times*, 27 May 2008.
6. *The Independent*, 25 May 2009.
7. *The Observer*, 24 May 2009.

Chapter 9

1. *Hansard*, 18 December 2007.
2. *Rudyard Kipling*, Charles Carrington, Macmillan, 1955, p. 155.

Chapter 10

1. *Daily Telegraph*, 8 December 2008.
2. Speech at the Open University, Milton Keynes, 26 May 2009.
3. *Daily Telegraph*, 22 July 2009.
4. *The Guardian*, 28 May 2009.
5. *Independent Member*, Methuen, 1950.

Chapter 12

1. *The Times*, 17 June 2009.
2. *Hansard*, 18 March 2003.
3. *Daily Telegraph*, 11 May 2009.
4. *The Independent*, 8 July 2009.
5. *Hansard*, 30 June 2009.
6. *Hansard*, 23 June 2009.

Chapter 13

1. Army Rumour Service, 19 June 2009.
2. Rum Ration, 11 July 2009.
3. *The Guardian*, 11 July 2009.
4. *Evening Standard*, 31 July 2009.
5. BBC News, 9 January 2007.
6. *Sunday Telegraph*, 12 July 2009.

7. BBC News, 22 July 2009.
8. Rudyard Kipling, 'Mesopotamia', 1917.
9. *Daily Telegraph*, 14 July 2009.
10. Rudyard Kipling, 'Epitaphs of the War', 1919.
11. *Daily Telegraph*, 17 July 2008.

Chapter 14

1. Evidence to the Kelly Committee, 23 June 2009.
2. Evidence to the Kelly Committee, 29 June 2009.
3. Committee on Standards in Public Life, 8th report, November 2002.
4. Evidence to the Kelly Committee, 29 June 2009.
5. Evidence to the Kelly Committee, 29 June 2009.
6. *Hansard*, 14 July 2009.
7. *Hansard*, 1 July 2009.
8. Report of the House of Lords Select Committee on the Constitution, 7 July 2009.
9. *Hansard*, 14 July 2009.
10. *Hansard*, 21 July 2009.
11. Evidence to the Kelly Committee, 16 July 2009.

Chapter 15

1. *Hansard*, 1 July 2009.
2. Evidence to the Kelly Committee, 11 May 2009.
3. Letter to the author, 13 July 2009.
4. Electoral Reform Society: Report of the Commission on Candidate Selection, September 2003.
5. *The Times*, 6 August 2009.
6. *The Plan*, Douglas Carswell and Daniel Hannan, 2008.
7. *The Truth That Sticks*, Icon, 2008, p. 28.
8. *New Statesman*, 6 July 2009.

Chapter 16

1. Speech to the Hansard Society, 30 November 2009.
2. BBC News, 1 December 2009.
3. *Daily Telegraph*, 30 October 2009.
4. *Daily Telegraph*, 30 October 2009.

5. Letter to Independents, the Independent Network, 1 January 2010.
6. *The Times*, 14 December 2009.
7. *Hansard*, 14 December 2009.

Chapter 17
1. William Cobbett, *Grammar of the English Language*, 1824.
2. *The Times*, 6 August 2009.
3. Evidence to the Kelly Committee, 16 July 2009.

Epilogue
1. *Daily Telegraph*, 5 February 2010.
2. Annual Report of the Committee on Standards in Public Life, 2 February 2010.
3. Evidence to the Public Administration Committee, 4 February 2010.
4. *Evening Standard*, 10 February 2010.

Index